There I Was...

Stories of Veterans From
WWI To The Present

Volume I

by

Peter A. Donnelly

THERE I WAS...
Stories of Veterans From
WWI To The Present

VOLUME I

Copyright 2016

Introduction

Greetings and welcome,

If you're reading this book you probably appreciate veterans, are a veteran, or you love a great story. This book, the first of many volumes to come, is a compilation of stories I've heard from other veterans. For the most part those stories were told over a drink in a bar or a cup of coffee in a diner. Some were heard over the phone and a few were written out by the storyteller. The range of time in service for the storytellers was from two years to over thirty. I wanted a casual setting so the vet didn't feel like they were being interviewed. I was also very careful not to lead them to tell me a particular story. If they had been awarded a medal for a conspicuous act, I didn't want them to think I necessarily wanted to hear that story. I did, but I wanted them to tell me whichever story they wanted. I knew most of the vet's backgrounds, so I was curious each time as to which story they would choose to tell, and sometimes I was surprised. Like I did, I want you to consider why that vet told that particular story.

The setup for each of the stories (except the ones I've included of deceased veterans) was to remind them that it was just them and me talking, to figure on about thirty minutes, and to simply tell me a story about their time in the service. There are some consistencies that became obvious in listening to these stories. Each one is full of emotion, a full range of emotions. The stories are diverse and there is a strong and noticeable ownership of each story by its teller. It belongs to that vet and sometimes that came with an equally noticeable sense of pride, and on occasion regret and remorse. You'll notice when you read the stories that they are presented as they were told, literally. I want you to feel like you are hearing it from them. If the story were read aloud from the page to you, it would sound like they were telling you the story. I didn't make any, well many, grammar or wording adjustments. I changed a few references and removed some names, but other than those minor edits, the rest is as it was told. This comes with some repetition, some "likes," and "uhs" and "ums" but that's the way people talk and I wanted the stories to read like friends and comrades talk to each other.

Two of the many motivations for me to create this series are actually two of the vets in this book. My Uncle Pete, as I'll detail later, served in World War II. You'll see through his story that he had an incredible wartime experience. When he came home he never talked about it, except this one story. I found out after he was gone, that he had written an entire book and had tried to get it published. He got frustrated with not being able to get his story told and toward the end of his life, took his book and threw it in a burn barrel and destroyed it. Those events, detailed with passion in that book are gone forever! My second vet motivator is Joe B. Joe is still going strong at 96. He told his stories with great passion in a voice from another time. As he says, "I'm writing for the living." Joe knows that his story needs to be told and even though he personally may have told it for the last time, he was ok with me doing it for him. So, I wanted to offer veterans an opportunity to tell their story, preserve our martial culture and the history of someone who served, in a simple way and save it, forever!

I feel capturing vets' stories this way, will give you, whoever you are and for whatever reason you're reading this book, an opportunity to share in the experiences of vets across all services, countries and numerous wars. For most of the stories I describe the setting and the drinks we were having. They are sequenced chronologically, by conflict. I really hope you enjoy this book, and those that follow and that you'll consider it a way to honor the teller of a story that meant a lot to them and may have been hard to tell. Our vets' stories need to be told and they need to be heard, so thanks for reading. And, read how you most enjoy reading, but for at least one of the stories, grab a drink; a beer, a glass of wine, a cup of coffee or tea and read the story like the vet is talking to you – because they really are.

THE GREAT WAR
1914-1918

World War I was horrible. It seems silly to feel the need to include the word "horrible" when describing a war, but there were many distinctions in The Great War that even make that word woefully inadequate in describing the horror and devastating impact the war had on all involved; the warriors, civilians, the land itself, the post war geopolitical situation, which led to World War II; everything. This post-Industrial Revolution war acted as a proving ground, on a grand scale, for new technologies developed to more effectively and efficiently kill people. The machine-gun would mow down millions across no-man's land. The airplane would strafe and drop bombs almost with impunity and give combatants another place to die for the first time in history, in the air. Poison gas would choke the life out of terrified soldiers or chemically burn them causing agonizing pain and a slow death. The flamethrower, although not new at the time of the war, was man-portable and incinerated entrenched enemies. The submarine was a new terror weapon aimed at the logistics of war, achieved by drowning or burning crews and passengers and sending their cargo to the bottom of the many oceans they hunted in. And, artillery; in World War I artillery was the greatest killer on the stagnant battlefield. It lived up to its moniker, "The King of Battle." New and sophisticated cannons, howitzers and mortars rained millions and millions and millions of shells down on the opposing forces. Shell shock became an identified condition and many thousands would suffer for the rest of their tortured lives, unable to revert back to the men they were before they participated and were broken in the Great War. According to the Encyclopedia Britannica[1], 8,500,000 were killed or died during the war. A total of 37,500,000 were casualties, which included wounded, captured and missing. With the overwhelming majority of casualties inflicted by artillery, many of the missing were probably disintegrated, blown to bits by one or several of the millions of shells fired in the four year conflict. There were several nations whose mobilized forces suffered incredibly. Austria-Hungary as an extreme example, suffered 90% casualties. The average casualty rate for the war was nearly 60%. It is impossible to calculate the full human toll the war had for those that survived; many to die in pain, confusion and sadness, not to mention the many who fought young and lived long enough to fight again in another global war, World War II. My grandfather was one who paid the price of 'Going Over There,' for the rest of his life.

---

[1] https://www.britannica.com/event/World-War-I/Killed-wounded-and-missing

Vet: *Peter*
Setting: *Gerity Funeral Home, Woodbridge, New Jersey*
Drinks: *None*

Story: This first story is one of the "one off" stories of the book. I'm telling it. I'm telling for, or more accurately, *about* my grandfather. I don't ever remember meeting him, and to the best of my recollection the first time, and the last time I ever saw him was when he was laid out in his casket at his funeral. I was seven. About eighty years separated us. He was born in the 1800's. I put it that way because it still amazes me that put broadly like that, the 1800's, includes a time that was over 200 years ago. That's about how long ago that day at the funeral home feels.

Peter was born in 1887 in a village somewhere in Romania. He immigrated to the United States and joined the Army in 1913, which is how he became a citizen. My grandfather served as a vehicle mechanic with the 4th Infantry Division, which was formed in December of 1917. The 4th deployed to France in June of 1918 and fought in the Second Battle of the Marne, Chateau Thierry, St Mihiel, Verdun and the Argonne Forrest. In 69 days of combat the 4th Infantry Division faced and fought eighteen German Divisions and took 1/20 of all American Expeditionary Force casualties of the war. During one of those battles he was wounded; gassed. Like many of the US soldiers returning from The Great War, his injuries weren't documented and would negatively affect the rest of his life. He married my grandmother, Josephine, in 1918. They had ten kids, five of them lived. One of them was my mom, the others were my Aunts, Judy and Theresa and my Uncles, Andy and Pete (his story is in the WWII section).

My grandfather spent most of the rest of his life in a VA hospital. He was seen as a difficult patient and argued with the staff and was eventually labeled as paranoid schizophrenic. With him in the hospital it was tough on my grandmother and their family. My Uncle Pete took over as head of the household and raised the kids. He became a professional boxer to pay the bills. They lost their house and were put on the street. My mom told me that, for a while, the staple for the family was lard sandwiches. She also told me they never got presents for Christmas, but one year she got the best Christmas present she'd ever get, an orange. To try and make ends meet and keep everyone together, my grandmother ran a small store. It was robbed once and she was beaten to within an inch of her life.

I don't know many of the details, but my grandfather languished for years suffering from the effects of his short tour in France during the Great War. He was in and out of the VA hospital for the rest of his life, and I never knew him. When my mom was a little girl, she still hadn't met her father so one day my aunts and uncles wrapped her in a blanket and snuck her into the hospital. When my grandfather saw her, he said, "I don't know you, I don't love you, never come back." That's all I know about my grandfather, a veteran of the Great War.

THE SECOND WORLD WAR
1939-1945

World War II was the largest most widespread conflict in world history. 3% of the planet was killed in war related circumstances, 60 million died. Some say that number is several times higher, and many times that number were casualties. Thousands and thousands died in the following years from the effects of the war; wounds, living conditions, starvation. And again the resolution of this war would lead directly or indirectly to future wars, which took many more lives. World War II was a truly industrial war, not only in war production but also in the strategic attacks on the industrial war machines themselves, factories, resources, workers, worker housing. Once again the world experienced technological advances that improved the efficiency and effectiveness of killing. The airplane as a war machine had become a sophisticated, powerful, deadly weapon, manufactured in numbers that would blacken the skies and will never be repeated. Tanks had evolved from monstrous, clunky, death traps to ever evolving hardened, big gun carrying assault weapons that spearheaded almost every campaign. Because of the demands of the war, industrial production advanced in four years what might have otherwise taken decades. The culmination of rapidly advancing technology in World War II was the atomic bomb. It is still amazing to me that in a world without computers and in an era where almost no one on the planet had a refrigerator, that man could develop the atomic bomb.

World War II always held a fascination for me. I grew up in the '60s and when we played outside, we played war, and we almost always played World War II. Our war toys were mostly World War II oriented, soldiers, tanks, planes, models, almost everything we played with was focused on World War II. Oh, GI-Joes, if you got a World War II GI-Joe, that was cool. They were actually making them for Vietnam around that time, but we were always fixated on World War II. It had only ended fifteen years before I was born. The guys in the bars my dad would take me to, those guys had fought in World War II, or Korea, so I heard the stories. My Dad's friend Mike was a tail gunner in a B-17 and told us that his life expectancy in combat was 19 seconds. But, he did his twenty-five missions and made it home. And there were all the good war movies of the '60s and '70s: The Longest Day; Tora, Tora, Tora; A Bridge Too Far; Bridge Over the River Kwai; Kelly's Heroes; The Great Escape; Twelve O'Clock High (That was an older one, 1949 – they had us watch scenes from it when I went to OTS in the early '80s), The Bridge At Remagen; the list goes on. We watched them all in the movies, usually with my Uncle Pete. I knew as I grew up and later when I served in combat that these movies were mostly glorification of war and some were barely historically accurate. But they did shape my early thinking. I knew I wanted to serve in the military and do something big, bigger than anything else. I wanted to do what my dad did, I wanted to do what my Uncle Pete did.

Someday soon, the guys who told those stories in the bars when I was a kid will all be gone. Someday soon, all of our World War II vets will be gone. My Uncle Pete is gone and he only ever told me one story about his service in World War II, and it was a good one.

Vet: *Pete*

Setting: *A Fall night in 1989 in the front yard of my parent's house in New Jersey. It was after our Thanksgiving meal. Me, my brother, my brother in law and my Uncle Pete were having beers and smoking cigars.*

Drinks: *Bud Lites all around.*

Peter Gatson, 276th Infantry Division, Germany, 1945

Story: My Uncle Pete was a great guy and spent a lot of time with my brother and me when

15

we were growing up. He never talked about his service in World War II, but on this particular night he opened up for the first time. Maybe it was because I had been in the military a few years by that point and maybe that changed the way he looked at his experience. I don't know, and he never talked about it again. He was a sergeant in the 276th Infantry Division, one of Patton's Divisions that were attacking into Germany. He led a mortar team. As the 3rd Army raced toward Berlin they were bypassing pockets of enemy forces. My Uncle found himself in a situation. The G2 had intel that at least a company sized, maybe more, element of Germans were following his company's line of advance. He didn't explain how this all happened, whether he volunteered, was ordered or if he made the decision to release the rest of his squad, but he was left behind to slow down the Germans, by himself. The area he was to defend was on top of a low hill. The approach to that hill was strewn with some trees, large rocks and undulating terrain. He picked a position near the top of the hill and set up his .30 Caliber Browning machine gun. It was still light out and he figured the Germans would reach his position after nightfall. He then told us that he sat down at the machine gun and thought. There were azimuth and elevation marks on the tripod. He took out his notebook and a stubby pencil. He looked out across the terrain and figured if he were attacking up this hill and started taking fire where would he hide. There was a fallen tree about three quarters of the way down the hill where the terrain started to level off. He aimed at it as deliberately as he could then squeezed off a short burst; hit low. He adjusted and fired another burst – right on. He wrote in his notebook:

  1. Fallen Tree – AZ 350 / EL 05

He did the same thing three more times; he figured he'd gotten the Kentucky-windage close enough and wanted to save his ammo and did the rest without firing to check his guestimates. By the time he was done he had a list of fifteen prime spots he would seek cover behind if he were the Germans. He also had a Thompson .45 caliber submachinegun. He had two ammo pouches with loaded magazines. One of us asked him if he taped the magazines together like they did in the movies. He laughed and said they didn't have tape back then. He put the Thompson and the magazines to the left of the machinegun tripod. He also had a satchel of grenades and put those next to the Thompson. There was a depression behind him that he could use for cover as a last stand position. He put his .45 colt and a couple of grenades in it in case he had to fall back and defend from there.

It was starting to get dark. He went through his aiming and reloading process over and over. He had four boxes of machinegun ammo. Pete opened them all lined them up side by side to the left of the machinegun. He had put the target list in order as he figured the Germans would progress up the hill, farthest first, closest last. He figured he had time for a can of rations and ate some peaches. He loved peaches and always ate them out of the can, as long as we knew him, which was all of our lives. He never put them in a bowl, he used a P-38 can opener, even in his house thirty some years later, and pried the lid back and always ate the whole can. Maybe it had something to do with that night. Maybe those peaches tasted really great because he thought they might be his last. We never knew, he didn't say.

He had rushed to get everything done before night fell, but now he was hurrying it on – he didn't want the Germans showing up, able to determine they were only facing one dogface on top of a hill. Luckily for Pete it got dark real fast.

My Uncle was a very calm, pragmatic guy and seemed generally happy, so it's hard to guess how he was feeling right at that moment, before the fighting started. He never expressed any emotions when he was telling this story; just what happened. I think sometimes if you've got a rough life, you might view situations like these differently, like it's another shitty situation you've got no control over and your choices are curl up in a ball and die or give it your best shot and see what happens. My Uncle had a rough life. At the time he was sitting on that hill in Germany he was twenty-nine years old and had been the head of his eight-person household for almost twenty years. Pete was Peter's son from the World War I story. So, he had received the life lesson of 'sucking it up' since he was a kid. I think that explains why he was up on that hill by himself. He figured the odds and as the squad leader he didn't see the point of risking his men, and wanted to take care of them, but not bringing them along.

So, now he waited. It had gotten quiet with nightfall. It wasn't long before he heard a different kind of quiet. The area was quiet, he heard no animal noises; the wind wasn't blowing. But, what he heard now was the quiet of the enemy trying to remain undetected as they moved toward him. Now he heard rustling leaves and twigs snapping; they were at the bottom of the hill. He told us at that point, he had to take a shit. He only had a minute or two, or maybe only a few seconds, but he decided this was more important than a hundred approaching Germans. He reached into his jacket pocket looking for toilet paper, but found a pair of spare socks. That gave him an idea. He took one of the socks and quickly drops his drawers and shit in it. This, he figured, solved two problems, he didn't have to move, and thus didn't have to worry about stepping in his own shit in the middle of a firefight. He could hear now that the Germans were getting closer. He had another hasty thought. He knotted the sock, swung it around his head and then launched it at the yet to be seen approaching enemy. 'Grenada!' came the response to the shit filled sock. That, Pete figured was as good a time as any, and he opened fire. He had the machinegun prepositioned to his first aim point and fired a short three round burst. The Germans came alive, shouting orders and returning fire. Pete knew the first few aim points by heart, so he kept up the fire, burst after burst. He threw a grenade a few dozen yards in front of his position, not seeing anyone to throw it at, but figuring it would kill the closest. He kept up the machinegun fire and the Germans were responding with everything they had. Pete now thought that just firing the machinegun would now give him away as a lone fighter. He grabbed the Thompson, took a few steps to the left and fired. He fired another burst from the machinegun, then stepped to the right and fired a prolonged burst from the Thompson. He got back on the machinegun and although in all the time I knew him I never heard him curse, I'd imagine at this point he probably said, 'Fuck it.' (He actually probably said 'to Hell with it') and started firing longer bursts with the machinegun. He'd gone through a couple of boxes of machinegun ammo already and was reaching for another when he got hit with a tracer round in the hand. It blew his hand back, but he again reached and retrieved the ammo box and reloaded. Several German grenades had gone off short of his position and wide left and right. His ruse was working so far. Just as he had fired at the last of the positions he documented in his notebook, he heard a thud, right next to him. For a split second he thought this was it; they'd figured out his position and a grenade just landed next to him. He looked down and didn't see anything at first, he fired again, figuring he could take a few more Germans out before he's blown to bits. Nothing happened. He looked down again, and could see now that it was his shit-filled sock. He laughed while telling us that part. I think he figured the Germans had a sense of humor, so maybe they'd appreciate that one American Army sergeant was at the top of the hill they were trying to take, holding off a hundred or so of them. I'm sure more happened, but Uncle Pete wrapped up the story by telling us that after some time, the enemy fire started to taper off. He shot a burst every few minutes, so they knew he was still there. Sometime between the height of the fighting and sunrise the Germans pulled back, what was left of them. When the sun came up Pete saw dozens of dead Germans lying around the positions he'd marked in his notebook. He left the machinegun, grabbed the Thompson and his pistol and moved out to rejoin his troops.

Pete survived the war. He continued to take care of his family, got a job in a chemical factory and worked there for forty years straight. He lived with his mother and brother in a 700 square foot house. He socked his money away; literally, he hid it in the rafters, heating ducts and floorboards of his small house. He never spent a nickel on himself and would give us five dollars whenever he'd visit. He never married, never had any kids, never went on vacation, but he seemed happy. Next to my dad he remains the most important figure in my life. Towards the end he didn't remember who I was, but I'll never forget him. I hope he looks down now and sees something of him in me.

****

Vet: *Joe B.*
Setting: *Joe's home in Newport News, Virginia*
Drinks: *Joe, orange juice. Me, a cup of Maxwell House coffee, black.*

Story: I met Joe in a veteran's writing group class sponsored by William and Mary University, held weekly on campus in Williamsburg, Virginia. I'd been a member of the Hampton Roads Veteran's Writing Group for a few years, but this session was the first one

I'd had in a class with Joe. Joe was from Brooklyn, New York, and was from the "Letter writing generation," as he put it. I just really enjoyed listening to him talk. He spoke with a rhythm and eloquence that highlighted that he'd grown up when grammar and vocabulary were more of an emphasis item in school. He built a career after his service as a schoolteacher and taught both in the US and in Germany, which I'm sure added to that style. Joe was, sorry, is a Marine. In thirteen months toward the end of the Second World War Joe fought in four invasions; Roi Namur, Tinian, Saipan and Iwo Jima. Joe has spent his life after the war telling his story. When I met Joe, he really didn't want to tell it anymore. It was a hard story to tell, but he told it, over and over. He knew people needed to hear it and to speak for those who couldn't tell their own version of it, because they didn't survive. One of those was his best friend, Joe Espisito. They were best friends and Joe B. joined because his friend did. Joe didn't want to tell his story anymore, but he was ok with me telling it for him, and for Joe Espisito.

Joe was born 23 August 1922. He enlisted in the Marine Corps and served from Feb 1943 through the end of the war, Dec 1945. Here's his story:

"I served in the central Pacific with the 4th Marine Division and participated in the invasion of Roi Namur in the Marshall Islands, Saipan, Tinian and Iwo Jima. My highest rank was PFC. It just happened to be that we were visiting cousins in Connecticut. My cousin at that time was working in a National Defense plan in New Britain Connecticut. My two older brothers were under the draft law and were standing by to enter the Army. While we were visiting we heard on the radio of the Japanese attack on Pearl Harbor. Naturally we were wondering if we were hearing correctly, but when they verified that the attack did take place certainly were stunned and wondered what the future would hold. I was about nineteen, just having graduated from high school. So, here's the situation, I had two brothers in the service. By the time my turn came, they were already in the service. We had to report to Church Street in New York City. They had all branches of the service recruiting at that time. My buddy, Joe Espisito from the neighborhood, told me that he got into the Marines. I was originally thinking of the Signal Corps with the Army, but somehow I was influenced by the recruiter. He played on my ego or something, telling me I was Navy or Marine material. So, since Joe had signed up, I just figured I'd be with him and found myself in the Marine Corps. Frankly, I didn't realize the full realization of what that meant.

The boot camp experience was very realistic and very rough. The first reaction I had was, why are they mistreating me this way? Everything was on the double and frankly, there was a question of harassment, what we thought were abuses and so on. But, then we started to realize that they were trying to do their best to give us this conditioning to strip us of our individuality, to realize you are a member of the team and the team and the platoon is what counts. With the training and the rifle range and the discipline and all the other things that came with it, we didn't fully appreciate boot camp, but then we realized that when we heard about Tarawa and the other experiences we realized they were trying to do their best to make sure we would fight and fight to survive. This was at Paris Island, South Carolina. After boot camp, you really felt privileged, you knew you were going to go into more advanced training. From there we went to Camp Lejeune, North Carolina and actually to Hadnod Point, which is a machine gun school, where we were familiarized not only with our rifles, the M1s, but, with machine guns and anti-aircraft weapons. We also had bayonet training and qualification. After Lejeune they were beginning to form some of the Regiments, like the 23rd and the 24th. We shipped out by troop train to the west coast and went to Camp Pendleton, Riverside, California. There we formed the 25th Regiment and then we activated the 4th Marine Division. Then we had ship to shore, more realistic training. We invaded Santa Catalina Island and some of the other islands off the Pacific coast. Very realistic with ships firing while we assaulted the beaches. Shortly after New Year's, around January 3rd or 4th we went out again, but this time we didn't come back so we knew we were headed out to a Japanese Island. We didn't know when we left shore, but rumor was that this was it. As the Marines say, "This is it."

While we were en-route, they pulled out large maps, three-dimensional maps and mentioned the 20th Marines would hit beach red or whatever it happened to be at the time. So, they told us very realistically what our objectives were and where we were going to land, where our beachhead was. We were outside of Pearl Harbor when our ships picked up the Navy and the other forces and then we were told it would be Roi-Namur in the Marshall Islands. They were small islands, but very concentrated. Roi was where the airfield was and was our main objective. Namur is where they had their installations. The objective of course was to get the airfield. This was the D-Day operation and there was quite a bit of resistance. My unit, the 20th Marines landed on Namur, which was the fortifications and the headquarters area. You have to remember, I was a private. I didn't have the 'Big Picture.' It was enough to know what our objectives were. With the Marines we talk about yards, not miles - therefore, it's only after that you learn the so-called, statistics. I believe there were about 13,000 Japanese. You have to remember that these were hard core Imperial Marines, seasoned troops. It was a complete military objective, we had to take over, or they had to push us back. It involved pretty close encounters. The islands were only about two miles each. If you make a diagram from where we are and make a circumference of two miles you realize the intensity and the closeness of the contact that was going to be involved. Most people don't realize the size of some of these islands. When you put your own troops against the enemy, I mean, you're bound to have close encounters – of the military kind. We eventually had 7000 going ashore. Although, I'm not so much schooled on the statistics, I'm seeing it from the private's point of view. Going over the side of the ship, you have a certain amount of assurance because the Navy is projecting their shells into the island and you're getting a certain amount of support. But, you still realize when you go down the nets; this is it. This is what all the training is for, the realistic training, the harassment, the discipline. You're young. Later on, especially on Iwo, you developed somewhat of a fatalistic attitude. In a way, that was helpful, because you were able to function. But, you always knew, you were at risk. The first encounter, yes, the adrenalin is up there, you really don't know what to expect, but then when you hit that beach you realize the firing is coming in your direction. I had an M1 rifle of course, a bandolier of ammo, of course your light pack with one set of fresh dungarees – we called them dungarees, I guess now you call them fatigues I guess, underwear, socks and of course a first aid kit and a gas mask. Unfortunately, for some reason, when the LCPVs approach the shore, they don't go flush up on the beach. They drop the ramp and we had to wade in. Unfortunately, the first night, it was cool, and with wet dungarees, it's very uncomfortable. We had to dig our foxholes too. We had what we called a two-man foxhole. Besides the night flares and the shelling, it was very uncomfortable, because we were all pretty wet. I learned this lesson and on Saipan we had to wade in, but this time I said, no, I'm not going to spend another night like that, wet and miserable. We were told to hold up as we were on the beach, so I jumped into a shell crater. I had my set of underwear and fresh dungarees in my knapsack and decided quickly to change in this shell hole and as I recall, we have this expression, 'A bare-ass Marine.' I certainly was a bare-ass Marine then. All of a sudden the sergeant says, 'Move up, move up!' and there I am stark naked in this shell hole. I know it sounds unbelievable, but this really happened. I never dressed so quickly in all my life. So, you see, you do learn, even those simple things.

The Japanese had aircraft on the island, but fortunately the shelling did considerable damage. But, this is early 1943 and we were subjected to nightly Betty attacks. As a matter of fact, they hit our ammo dump. If they dropped a bomb with a full moon, they were going to hit something. In the early stages, they did hit our ammo dump. Other than making the landing and facing a certain amount of mortar and rifle fire, as a matter of fact, I went into a crater and without exaggeration, in the crater was a dead Jap. That was my first experience seeing a dead enemy and unfortunately, later dead Marines. We had secured Namur and we helped out on Roi. We were combat engineers. When they hit our ammo dump, Ken and I were trapped. We dug under a bulldozer on Namur and the spent shells were all around us. The fact was we scraped and crawled and fortunately the bulldozer blade was down. It was like being in an empty shell, the small arms fire was ricocheting off the blade. We had to make a choice, should we run for it? We knew our tanks were a little forward and Ken says, 'Let's run for it.' There were concussions from everything going off. Frankly, it was a miracle that we made it.

I ended up with a tank group. Now it's night. We were separated from my platoon. When dawn came, we were able to go back to our unit. As a matter of fact we were reported missing, because we hadn't shown up. Eventually we get back to the platoon area and I was glad to see my buddies, Ozzie and Bill and Joe and Stan. That was my first combat experience, and that proved the realities of war and that some things were out of your hands and out of your control.

The term, 'seasoned' veteran. Each campaign has its unique battle characteristics. You learn each time, but what made us go out the second time? What made us go out the third time, because we invaded Tinian after Saipan? What made us go out the fourth time? I don't know. You may call it the Esprit de Corps. You don't want to let your buddies down. That's why I mentioned the word fatalism. There was an element of fatalism that entered as you became a seasoned veteran. So, you were going to do that dirty job, try to get it over with and hope to survive.

During the bombing of our ammo dump I really thought I wasn't going to survive. That was the real test. I began to realize what the realities were; it hardened you because you began to realize you had to kill so that they don't kill you. That old phrase, kill or be killed. That night, we had forty casualties, I didn't want to mention all those other details; we had forty casualties. Not all dead, but we had forty casualties that first night. You see, the island is very small. It's amazing when you think of it in retrospect, the concentration that was taking place on a relatively small island. You think about all of that concentration of fighting, what was it for – it was for the airfield! That was the objective. They were willing to sacrifice.

Roi-Namur was a short operation, as a matter of fact the battle only lasted three days and three nights. Relatively speaking that was rather a successful baptism of fire for us, because we were able to take over the islands in that short time. I have to give the Japanese due respect. They were terrific fighters; they didn't want to be captured. Many of them committed suicide, Hare Kari. They put the rifle under their chin. It was a disgrace for them to be prisoners. I've got other experiences, especially on Iwo, with the few prisoners we had, the enemy was firing on their own men because they considered it a disgrace that we even had a few prisoners in the stockade along the beaches of Iwo. I have to commend them. They were fanatic fighters but they fought.

I was so happy to get off that island, as we all were naturally. We were relieved by the Army and the Seabees. Being a kid from Brooklyn, not that I was the platoon clown or anything, but I was so relieved to get off that island when we passed by the Army and the Seabees as they came ashore I walked around as if I was lost and I said, 'Pardon me Mac, which way is it to boot camp?' We were picked up by a merchant marine ship that had unloaded supplies and whatnot and they claimed that they were short of food. They didn't anticipate picking up as many Marines aboard. It was bad enough on the island, we had K rations and C rations, but aboard ship, believe it or not we only had soup and sandwiches. But, I noticed something, and there's one thing I can say about the Marine Corps, they train you well. But they also train you how to take care of yourself. I'm not saying they teach us to cheat and to steal, but they teach us to survive, in all occasions. I noticed on the deck the smell of food was good. Because of the bombing, I lost my sea bag too. So, the Navy gave me blue denims, blue dungarees. So, when I was on the ship it was like I was part of the crew. I went up there and believe it or not, I was able to have a meal on the bridge of the ship. I went down below and I said, 'This is great.' But then I risked it. I went up for dinner and a Chief Petty Officer asked me, 'Hey, where do you work?' And I said, 'I'm down in the engine room,' figuring they don't know who works down in the engine room. He says, 'Look Mac, you get your ass off this bridge and I don't want to see you ever again.' So, with that I got the knife, got the butter, put it on the bread and took a big bite and said, 'Thanks, but no thanks.' I had to go down below. It's a good thing he didn't put me on report. I can talk lightly about it now, but really, aboard ship I was even looking at garbage cans, that's how - well C rations and K rations are not very nourishing. And also, knowing that there was food aboard, you get desperate.

Aboard ship some of us broke out in amebic dysentery. I talked about the smallness of the island. Along with the Jap dead and our dead and the heat and the flies and the corrosion and the deterioration and mind you, you don't bury your dead and you certainly don't take care of the Japanese dead. You take care of your own casualties and your own dead. Anyway, the island was infested with flies and maggots. Obviously some of us were contaminated and I broke out with amebic dysentery. And that's the most painful, humiliating type of agony that you could go through. You're in pain, you void, you are in no condition; you actually wish you could die. It's almost like a mortal wound.

When we got to Maui in the Hawaiian Islands, which was going to be our advanced base, we were going to set up tent camps on Maui at the base of Mount Haliaka. They took us right off the ship and naturally they took care of the casualties, the wounded and there was such an overflow on this little island and the military hospital that they took the dysentery and the other cases into the high school gym. And they had us on the floor of the high school gym. They set up a field hospital in the high school to take care of us. So, I experienced amebic dysentery and even today I don't like any jokes that deal with the stomach or eliminations or anything of that type because it's no laughing matter. No laughing matter. Fortunately, being in good condition after a while I was able to recover. The funny thing was, when we were in this high school gym, the Red Cross women came and wanted to give us reading material and of course the only reading material they had for the most part were woman's magazines. It was comical to see these combat Marines reading Women's Home Companion, but in those days they had good short stories. Not like the women's magazines, and I'm not being sexist when I say this, but the emphasis on these magazines is much different that it was in the '40s and '50s.

I hate to use the term, but they made us crap out for a week, just to rest. Light drill and watch and whatnot. Then, we got briefed, because we had to relearn what we learned from Tarawa, the other Division's experiences, plus our experiences on Roi-Namur. Therefore the training became even more intensified. As combat engineers we worked out more with demolitions then we did previously. Satchel charges, so the emphasis was going to be on demolitions, along with other duties. Now there's something about combat engineers that maybe I'd like to explain. Certainly your training is geared toward clearing mines and most people don't know this, because we're talking a number of years ago, a half-century and beyond, but when we hit the beaches, we had to probe with our bayonets for mines. We laid a strip of tape so those that followed us would know at least that supposedly that was a safe avenue. But in the confusion of combat you can't always do that. You've got more landing behind you; you've got to keep moving. Anyway, they knew the next operation was going to be a larger island with more beachhead. We built the tent camp. We had four Marines per tent. We laid out the rifle range. The training was intensified.

It was only three and a half months and we were ready to invade Saipan; Saipan in three and a half months. We had a little bit of liberty every other weekend to go into the town of Aiuku, but there was nothing there. I had an allotment. I was only a private, twenty one dollars a month, but I still had an allotment for my family, for my parents, because you know, the seven or eight dollars you had for liberty, you know, there wasn't even any women to socialize with. It was a case of maybe going in there and having a Hawaiian steak and a beer. That was our liberty. Fortunately though I had a Captain Stone, who was interested in the arts and he formed a little art group at the local USO. And we used to go there and sketch; unfortunately we didn't have any nude models in those sessions.

In three and a half months we're heading to Saipan. The heavy shelling was kind of an assurance but people have to realize that that shelling doesn't do as much damage as we think it does, because those Japanese were entrenched. Of course, this is a big island too. The shelling is mostly on the beaches and a couple of miles beyond, because of course they want to ensure the security of the landing of the Marines. We had to wade in again and they opened up a little more because of course they had the beaches secured. They knew where we were going to land, or where we had to land, the most feasible area. We hit a compound that housed Japanese torpedoes and bombs and that really exploded and the vapors and smoke came in our direction, so this is the first time, through all our campaigns that we had to resort to our gas masks. And this is maybe D+3, D+4, so we were pretty much in the interior, beyond the beachhead. I donned my gas mask and I couldn't breathe and I was wondering what was wrong. I examined my gas mask and realized the canister was corroded from the salt water because we had waded in and unfortunately I had my gas mask holder a little lower than my knapsack. I was desperate because, really the fumes were evident. I crawled into another area and there was a dead Marine and fortunately his gas mask was ok, it was dry, so I used it. I don't want to be literary, but it was like the dead serving the living. Whether you're trained or not, the unexpected happens. The unexpected happens. Roi-Namur was strictly a military objective, no civilians involved. It was military against military, Marine against Japanese soldiers and Imperial Marines. Saipan, we were going to be involved in towns like Garapan. There were sugar can factories and things like that. So, after we secured a smaller town, Chalan Kanoa, we infiltrated Garapan, which had the Japanese headquarters there. We were involved in town fighting and this involved what you might call street fighting.

One night in the town of Garapan while the campaign was still going on we cleared some debris. When you reach a point before darkness, you pull back and set up your perimeter, so at least you know what's in front of you twenty-five yards. When we were setting up we were fired upon. Joe DeCosta and I fire back in the area in the darkness. There were two Japanese that we killed. When we approached them we realized one was a woman. And this is another thing we didn't count on; that we were eventually going to deal with women. There's much more to that story that I don't care to relate. It's natural to see the enemy dead and even our own dead, but when we saw that first woman, you realize that we were going to encounter...of course we couldn't see into the future but I want to mention this. I'm sure in future wars like Korea and Vietnam, they had to deal with this, they couldn't trust anyone, man, woman or child.

On the lighter side, when we went through Garapan, there was a home that was demolished. I came across a wonderful Jap wooden sculpture of a fisherman. Because of my art background and art education and training, because I graduated from the High School of Music and Art in New York City, I took it. It was like a symbol of sanity, creativity amid all that destruction. I put it in my knapsack. The next morning we got the order to move up. We start moving out and I felt like, oh my God this is a burden, so I thought I'll put it in this hole here and maybe on the way back I'll pick it up. This brings up the idea of souvenirs. Marines, many of them, liked to collect souvenirs; bloody Jap flags, Samurai swords, Jap pistols, whatever. But, we were not only told, but we had incidents where they would booby trap their dead. They knew some would search for souvenirs. But I never went for that, not even during the campaigns. As a matter of fact, if you were to visit my home you wouldn't even know that I was in the Marine Corps. You don't see anything in my house, not even my honorable discharge papers and other things. Yeah, I have some photo albums, but I mean in terms of, not that I was ashamed of what I did, the point is, is that I didn't have that kind of interest or mentality to pursue things like that. But, my friend Joe Esposito, on Saipan his platoon came back with quite a few souvenirs and he had them. But here's the situation, and I don't want to discredit anybody, but I have to tell the truth. As we were relived and we went back to the beachhead, a jeep pulled up with a Navy officer. He had in this jeep, beans, hot bread, mind you we were still on C rations. 'Okay Gi-rines take out your Jap pieces.' We're going to exchange and barter and Joe Esposito, we're hungry as all hell; he gave up some of his souvenirs. He had loaves of bread and so on and he came to me, we were relieved at the same time, his platoon and mine. Being a neighborhood buddy, Joe came to me and he said, 'Here I want to share this with you.' 'Joe,' I said, 'Your platoon earned it, I appreciate the thought of it, but please share it with your platoon.' I hate to say this, but I don't know, I hope that Navy officer survived the war and maybe he's got these Japanese souvenirs in his den, and I hope so. But, I just hope he doesn't tell false stories about how he obtained them. The tragic part, and we didn't know at that time, and I'm not trying to be literary, but this idea of Joe giving loaves of bread, it was almost a religious, Christ-like gesture, because Joe was killed on D-Day on Iwo Jima. He was killed on D-Day on Iwo Jima.

Here again now, Saipan, if I remember correctly, is about thirteen and a half miles long. Tinian was the next island, only two and a half miles separated from Saipan. When we talk in terms of time elements, some people would say, 'Gee it only took thirty six days to take over Saipan?' But they don't realize it's thirty-six days and it's thirty-six nights and it's constant! It's constant! There's no real let up. Whether you have the 14th Artillery howitzers, they're moving up too. When the tanks come ashore, and we don't have heavy tanks, we have these light tanks, Sherman tanks. We're moving, constantly. Anyway, we didn't realize we had to invade Tinian too, but since the Saipan operation was secured, we call it secured. We realized we needed Tinian. It was more of a rectangular island and it had a longer airfield. For the first time, we were able to set up 155mm Howitzers at the northern tip of Saipan and shell Tinian. Of course we had Naval support, but this is the first time this type of operation took place. Tinian knew what was happening on Saipan. They were ready for us. And they knew that they had to fight to the death. Tinian, even though it didn't get much exposure in history that was a very terrific campaign. Fortunately we did get Tinian, as you know later when we built the airfield, that's where our B-29s were able to take off to bomb Japan.

After Tinian we headed back to our advanced base in Maui in the Hawaiian Islands. There again we had about a week to recoup. There we were able to eventually, like the other campaigns, we had orientations to learn about things we should be doubly aware of with our experiences on Saipan and Tinian. Of course, we try at this time, along with the training, to have more of a recreational set up. The rumor was that after Tinian and Saipan that we were going to be heading stateside, or that we'd be getting some leave. But unfortunately, it was only a rumor. In the Marine Corps it seems R & R, which means Rest and Recreation, in the Marines it means Replacements and

Replacements. Therefore that rumor was killed in the bud and we regrouped, retrained and we were now assigned to the different regiments. The combat engineers, we worked with the 23rd Regiment in one campaign, the 24th Regiment in the Saipan/Tinian campaign and the 25th we found out we were going to work with them on the next one, which was Iwo Jima. This time the camp, although primitive, was a little more set up than the previous times we set up our tents. They had a baseball field, or the equivalent, and a few more recreational activities for us. We had a boxing ring too and fortunately once in a while a USO troop would come. So, even though we were very primitive, still in tent camps, outdoor movies sitting on sandbags and if it rained it didn't bother us, we were used to rain, we're used to having rain even in our foxholes. Then, as I said, after Saipan, the demolitions seem to get special emphasis. Prior to our invasion of Iwo, of course we didn't know it at this time it was going to be Iwo, but they realized that the Japanese were going to be well fortified. They had a system of caves and tunnels and underground entrenchments, pillboxes and things of that type. As we get closer to the mainland, if you study a map of the south Pacific, Saipan is quite close to the mainland of Japan and Iwo was only 750 miles from the mainland. So, the concentration was more on demolitions, satchel charges, Bangalore torpedoes, I mean it was getting so that the emphasis was on the demolition of fortifications, of Jap entrenchments. Now, even though we had what you would call the combat experience, we also had heavy casualties, heavy casualties.

So, it was a question of replacements. Prior to the Iwo campaign we were sometimes getting members who were wounded on Guadalcanal with the 1st Marines, or the campaigns of the other Marines, they would come in as replacements. In a way, we had more experienced troops, but without quoting a General, the General said, 'One Marine Division that has seen combat is worth two Divisions stateside.' So, it was replacements and replacements and we weren't going to go on any home leave or anything.

Here's the situation from my personal experience and viewpoint on the landing. As we were approaching Iwo Jima with our troop ships and assault boats and destroyers, with the Navy accompaniment naturally, we were in zigzag formation, obviously, throughout. If you'll note, you study from where we left in Maui in the Hawaiian Islands we had to pass the Marshall Islands, we had to pass the Marianas, which is Saipan and Tinian and we had to continue on to Iwo Jima. We're talking about a considerable number of sea miles, in zigzag formation. Anyway, the night before D-Day, it was about 0245 in the morning. We were assigned hatch watches and I had just gotten off of a two-hour watch on deck. Down below was the troop compartment and unfortunately it always seems, being a PFC, at this point I had been promoted, you get the bad deal. The bunks were low to the ground and very congested and generally next to the latrines or the heads, many of them were malfunctioning and the swirl would come right below and if you had a lower rack you were in for it. In some cases I'd go topside and sneak into one of the life rafts to get some fresh air and so on. I was always discovered in the morning by the SPs or the officer of the day on watch, of course. Getting to the D-Day invasion, I just got off watch, I was just about to take my boots off and hit the sack, when the ship got a terrific impact. We thought, this is it, Jap torpedo; we caught a fish! 'Man your battle stations!' 'Man your boarding stations!' I must say this, and once again, not because it's the pride of the Marines, but even in this crisis situation, there was not any real panic. I mean we all rushed topside and the ship started to list. In the thick of night, 0245 in the morning, the landing craft on the starboard side could not disembark because of the angle of the ship. Fortunately, my station was on the portside of the ship, the left side. Some Marines jumped in because they thought... Later we found out, it was in the zigzag formation, our ship had gotten too close to another and they rammed each other and by some miracle they were able to close off the compartments, because the compartment were flooded and that's what gave the ship the list. Then a destroyer pulls up and throws a light on our nets and we thought this time we were really going to catch a Jap fish because we were right off of Iwo. Fortunately, things got pretty much under control. They were able to rescue those that had jumped overboard. We had to stay aboard ship. D-Day was the next morning. The 20th Marines, combat engineers, of course our section, there's Company A, Company B, and so forth. We weren't able to get off. This is the first operation I was in that I wasn't involved in D-Day, because, after D-Day, they came back and were able to take us off the ship and we went in D + 1, early.

Now, here it is. The Japs let us get on the beaches, there was still mortars and artillery, but for the most part, they let us get onto the beaches. But they had a reason. They knew where we landed was the only possible places to land. They had that area zeroed in from the northern end of the island to Suribachi. We knew we were going to be caught in a crossfire; a crossfire, from Suribachi to the northern end. Our objective was Moriyama Airfield Number 1, which was short distance from Suribachi. And they zeroed in for the first week or so. On D+ 2, D+ 3 the weather turned against us. The rough seas disrupted all our craft and we had to sit and basically take it. Now the 14th Artillery pieces, our 75s were active rain or shine, but for the most part, the engineers and a good part of the infantry were pretty well bogged down, in our foxholes and just taking it. And that's why we also had heavy casualties. You really couldn't dig what you would call the traditional type of foxhole because it would cave in on the sides because of the loose volcanic soil, ash. Fortunately, I'm not of a tall stature, so any kind of a hole or crater would suffice for me. But then I learned that Joe Esposito landed on D-Day and was killed. Now in the early phases of the operation we can't bury out dead right away. So, when we were holed up, no more than about fifty yards or so, under a poncho was my buddy, Joe Esposito, under the poncho, in the rain. I couldn't do a thing; I couldn't do a thing for him.

Fortunately we also had the 5th Marines. At this time there was a 5th Marines and this was going to be their first combat experience. But, they were responsible for Suribachi. They were responsible to cut through that island, and of course, naturally with our assistance because we were shelling Suribachi too of course. Fortunately, it was D+3 or 4; they were able to secure Suribachi. Mind you, this is another small island. Saipan was thirteen and a half miles; Iwo Jima is only what, five and a half by eight miles; at the most. And you had heavy compliment of Marines and 23,000 Japanese. When that flag went up, and really I saw that flag go up, I saw that flag go up and just like a bunch of kids like we were at a football game. You could hear firing in the air, you could hear boat whistles and sirens, you could hear everyone so excited about the fact that we supposedly secured Suribachi. And also we knew, hopefully, we're no longer trapped under a crossfire. There's still always enemy activity, whether you put up a flag or not, but we knew at least we could concentrate now in the forward position toward the northern end of the island. But still, they zeroed in on us. And I'm not exaggerating, no matter where you were on this island, you might think the beaches by day four, five, six or seven, were safer, no. Because, from the caves, and I'm not exaggerating and I'm sure history will prove me right. One night I counted at least nineteen to twenty rockets from the caves. We called them buzz bombs then but that term has a different significance today. They would drop just about anywhere, on our positions. That was the uncanny thing, to see them. Now fortunately, in a way, they kind of exposed themselves from the caves when they shot these rockets. This time out we had destroyers coming in closer and cruisers coming in closer and they would support us by shelling these areas. I'm not going into the specific details, because frankly, I was only involved in five yards at a time. I didn't see the big picture. We realized how dug in the Japanese were. Because even during daylight, lots of time you didn't come across mass troops like we did on Saipan and Tinian, in terms of Japanese tanks and counterattacks of that type. No they did most of their fighting at night and they were terrific night fighters. The caves were natural and hollowed out. Remember, the Japanese had these islands, if I recall correctly, this I only learned much later, they had these islands for over ninety years. Iwo Jima was considered part of their mainland and they knew as the war progressed, they knew that they had to fortify that island. Now the rumor was we were going to invade Formosa, but the Navy was against that. They wanted to go direct and they needed it because we were losing our bombers taking off from Saipan and Tinian and Iwo had a radar station that alerted the mainland so they knew when our bombers were coming over. And we had terrific loses. Japanese fighter planes would take off out of Iwo and cut our planes down if they were half crippled, or didn't have enough gas, so we had terrific loses. Now there's one thing I'd like to say, and this is memory of the Marines who sacrificed themselves. I'm talking about this particular campaign since we're talking about Iwo Jima. It was proven that by getting Iwo, even though the war was going to end months later, that we saved, must have been about 30,000 crew and pilot lives, Air Force lives, by taking Iwo Jima, although we lost 6000 dead, just for that little island. Twenty-six days and twenty-six nights; you talk to people and they think, 'Gee, that wasn't much...' Concentrated! Day and night! No matter where you were, killing, you couldn't bury your dead; you didn't worry about the Jap dead. Because of the heavy weaponry we experienced from their fortifications we had more mutilation, more torn up bodies, then we ever experienced on Saipan or Tinian or any of our previous operations. Everything was so concentrated.

The few prisoners we took, we set up a little stockade on the beach. The enemy shelling was too accurate; they killed the few prisoners we had. There were not many prisoners to be taken. When we were clearing, and eventually we had to dig with the bulldozers, but look, we didn't worry about MOS, I wouldn't say, 'Hey I'm just supposed to clear mines...' No, we had a lot of things to do on Iwo. We were called to assist the infantry, even the artillery, whether it was to bring up ammo, or water, or to help with the reinforcements, sandbagging certain artillery installations. Many of the corpsmen were killed; we had to assist with the wounded. I remember we said, on the island, 'If we get hit, let's get hit during the day,' because evacuation might be more readily available. You get hit at night it's a different story. Also, most people don't know the ships pull out, especially at night because they're targets, and they had to protect the area because there were still some engagements at sea. But fortunately they came back at early dawn, LSTs for the supplies and the ammo. But that time I mentioned with the rain we couldn't get any supplies in. The surf was so heavy it destroyed a lot of our equipment. The tractors couldn't even get on shore in the early stages because the soil composition was not conducive. We had to lay this grated metal mats so the tractors could go forward on them.

Then we got Moriyama airfield. Then we were able to get more ammo and supplies and troops and Seabees. I have to give credit to the Navy SeaBees. Mature men, skilled and trained, and they're the ones that helped out getting the airfield. Believe it or not, we were able to get some of the fighter planes that were giving us low level support to land on Moriyama and then just take off from Moriyama, drop their loads with in a few minutes and then land back on the airfield, miraculous. There were three airfields on Iwo, Moriyama was the main, Moriyama #2 was pretty well constructed and then there was a third one, which was in the process of being constructed. At night, one or two Bettys, we called them Bettys would come through and drop their loads. That's another thing, being a small island like on Roi-Namur, being a small island, no matter where they dropped they were going to hit something. And we cursed the full moon! We cursed the full moon! Because we knew we were definitely going to get air attacks. The silhouette of the island with the fluorescent ocean was a perfect target.

After twenty-six days, we were relieved by the Army and we got more Seabees. Fortunately, we went back to Maui. We made a lot of trips to Maui, of course we were with the fleet Marines, but I'll tell you I think we had more sea duty than the average sailor in World War II. You study your maps and you realize we're talking the distance from Maui to Roi-Namur, 3479, don't quote me, but over 3000 sea miles, just to Roi-Namur. Then you go to Saipan, which is further west, and mind you, you don't get off the ship. I want to mention an incident. When we invaded Roi and Namur the Seventh Army invaded Kwajalein, another part of the Marshall Islands, Eniwetok, Pari Island and so on. My older brother, my oldest brother, my brother Al, unfortunately he's passed away; he was with the Seventh. When we secured Roi and Namur he was able to get a supply boat, he was a sergeant – in the Army, you get promotions. You just have good conduct for six months – you get a stripe, but not in the Marine Corps. You have to drill a platoon, you have to know your manual, you have to do a lot of other things before you get your stripe! Anyway, they had relieved us. Now, I had just gotten on a merchant ship. My brother came to Roi and Namur, this may sound a little surprising, he asked them, 'Do you know Joe Bruni?' And they did, because the Marine Corps, we're a small unit, comparatively speaking. We work so close together. I knew my buddies better than my brothers; I have to admit. We have a close bond. And they drill that into you, the teamwork, they strip you in boot camp of your individuality, your personality, there's the teamwork and if somebody goofs on the platoon you're all punished, not just KP, but you had to scrape out toilets with a toothbrush. I talked to some young Marines and they said there is the harassment, but they said they don't believe they could treat us like they treated your generation. But anyway, it was unfortunate I was not able to have a reunion with my brother. I did late meet up with my brother on Parris Island and we had an emotional reunion. We looked out at all the ships and he said, 'Man, you're in for a big one.' He didn't tell me until well after the war, but he didn't think he'd ever see me again. He knew we were closed to the mainland and he had experienced combat.

After Iwo, again we went back to Maui and the regrouping. I was assigned to another unit, which was definitely demolitions. After you get that combat experience your job gets tougher and tougher. Here something unusual happens. Five of us were selected to go to Okinawa. If you know your history, the Iwo Jima campaign ended in late March, early April. The invasion of Okinawa was April 1st, around Easter time. So, they had secured the islands, the Army and Marines invading Okinawa. Only a month after getting back from Iwo, they assign five of us special duty and we thought it was TDY, temporary duty to go to Okinawa because they were getting raids on Yontan airfield near Naha on Okinawa. When we got back, we were really in training for the invasion of Honshu and Kyushu. That was going to be an all-Marine operation. As combat engineers we were known as camouflage specialists. We were supposed to camouflage the anti-aircraft batteries on Yontan airfield. But I don't know, frankly it's a mystery why they pulled five of us. In a way, I have to be honest. After the experiences we had, especially on Iwo, I must admit I felt somewhat relieved. But then there was the bond. Even though they said it was temporary, I still want to be with my Division. I want to still be with my unit, with my buddies, or the survivors of my buddies. But at the same time, it was a mixed emotion, I felt kinda relieved. Because I knew I was going to be assigned to an anti-aircraft battery, that's what the orders read. I know I'd be taking a chance there too, but it's not going to be with the invasion of Honshu and Kyushu. And I'm attached to Company A, strictly demolition squad. And I thought, what could we possibly do, teach them to make these string nets, camouflage foliage?

Then we heard on the Jeep radio, Tokyo Rose, she mentioned a lot of things, she seemed to be very knowledgeable of what was going on with our units and campaigns and so on. Then we heard about the Atomic Bomb, because of course I was out there in August. Well, we thought, ok, big bomb. Then we heard there was a second bomb. We didn't realize the full extent, frankly. When we heard about the end of the war, even though we heard propaganda from Tokyo Rose, and we got it from the commanding officer, when we heard about the end of the war. It was like the time on Suribachi, at nearby Yontan airfield you could hear all the firing in the air and so on, we were so relieved that the war was ended. But, then they wanted Marines to volunteer to disarm the Japanese in China. I said, 'no, no, no, I survived this much, by the grace of God, and whatnot, no, I'm ready. I've got enough points'. We had the point system; I got enough points to go home tomorrow. I'm not going to go there, we had enough Japanese after the war still killing Army on Saipan and in these other places, they didn't give up, even if the war was over. I wasn't going to be knocked off by some Japanese in China who didn't want to get the word. Now coming back though from Okinawa we still had blackout even though the war was over. We were worried about these fanatic Japanese submarines. So, I was on Okinawa with the artillery group when the war ended, when they dropped the bomb.

For Saipan we received the Presidential Unit Citation and for Iwo we had the second Presidential Unit Citation. Fortunately, and for some miracle I can't understand because better men then me on my right, on my left, behind and in front of me got hit. But I mentioned on the first night on Roi-Namur we had forty casualties. I got concussion, I got near escapes and things of the type, but I was not wounded. I was not wounded. But, I have to admit this and I realize this is on tape, but on Iwo when we were trapped, I had almost the rifle to my foot, during daytime, once. It was just a moment of insanity, but that's all it takes, a moment of insanity. But, I didn't do it. I didn't do it. Not because I was a hero and I certainly didn't think I was a coward, I just said I'm going to trust, and I can't let my buddies down. Crazy.
I kept a lot of things internally, which I don't think was very good, although I wasn't aware of it. Fortunately I was able to come home to a

warm family. To a friend and a good neighborhood with a mixed ethnic makeup, we knew each other, others who having also survived."

"I was at the nets, ready for the invasion, this is no slur on the other services, but, there was another young sailor who was assisting with the nets who says, 'Oh, you Marines, you get all the glory.' I said, 'Mac, I'll tell you what; you want to trade places with me now? I'd be more than happy to do so.' That's why I'm saying I had enough glory. I'm here for Joe Esposito because I personally knew him and we got into the Marine Corps together. I'm here to represent all services and all men who fought all our wars."

Joe's creative instincts were rekindled when he got back from the war. His brother had used the GI Bill and got a scholarship, he was also interested in the arts. This inspired Joe to go to art class at the Brooklyn Museum; it was like art therapy. He went to Pratt Institute in Brooklyn and got a two-year degree attending in the evenings. He was now twenty-three or twenty-four and felt a bit like a kid again, because he had to start over again. He got an apprentice job in an ad agency and worked with some art directors and continued to study at night. All his friends were getting married and "bringing bambinos into the world," as he puts it. He fell in love a couple of times but didn't think he could support a family on $42.50 a week.

Joe always had in the back of his mind the thought of seventeen and eighteen year old lives snuffed out, so short and thought there had to be more to life, so he thought, "I gotta get an education." Joe's dad was an immigrant and served in World War I, that's how he got his citizenship. Joe was a survivor and he was still working to survive. He went on to the New York University School of Art Education, again attending at night and continued working hard and studying hard and eventually obtaining his teacher's license and taught for three years in the New York public school system. The first school he taught at had 3000 students, and it was a rough school, he always thought he was hired there for his military experience, "certainly not for my stature." He always believed his Marine Corps experience made him "stick it out," and to know that you have to continue to sacrifice if you have a goal.

Joe got a teaching job with the Department of Defense overseas and taught on military installations in Germany. That's where he met his wife. She was somewhat younger than Joe and had experienced war as a young girl. That shared experience created a lasting bond, which continues to this day.

The Korean War
1950 – 1953

On June 25th, 1950, North Korea, aided by Communist China invaded South Korea with the goal of reunifying the Korean peninsula under communist rule. On June 27, 1950 the United Nations responded to the invasion and directed a coalition of twenty-one countries to defend South Korea. Almost 90% of those forces were US. Over the course of the war approximately 2.5 million people were killed. It could be argued that the Korean War was a direct result of the political decisions made at the end of World War II. A formerly unified nation was divided both geographically and politically. Korea saw the first jet to jet combat and some of the armaments from World War II were still effective enough to rain death and destruction on the participants; B-29s, B-26s, most of the naval vessels and some tank models were employed throughout the war. The helicopter was first used effectively, but trench lines and fixed fortifications still found their way back into the modern war, the first US hot fight of the Cold War. The battle lines swung back and forth across almost the full length of the opposing sides. The intervention of masses of Chinese forces ended hopes for a UN victory when nearing the Yalu River. A stalemate ensued and an eventual cease-fire and armistice was agreed upon on July 27th, 1953. The US lost approximately 35,000 killed during the three-year war.

Vet: *Bob*
Setting: *Kitchen Table*
Drinks: *Bob, Budweiser, me, Guinness Pub Draft.*

Story: "I was on the American Submarine, USS Requin SSR- 481 as an Engineman 3rd Class. At one time I was told that I was the youngest throttle man in the Navy. (I was told that only 10% of sea stories must be true.) On the surface I ran the engines in the after engine room. When we dove I would shut down my engines and haul ass to the control room to man the trim manifold. What I did, on orders from the dive officer, was move water from trim tank to trim tank to fine tune the boat to a level state. I could do this by changing valves and using air, or a pair of pumps, to move water from one tank to another. Some of the guys would drive a new dive officer nuts by having 10 guys drift to the bow and wait until the officer would get the trim set, then, one by one, drift aft until the bow would head up.

We were in the Mediterranean in early February 1951, operating with the Italian Naval Forces out of Taranto, Italy. We were with the United States 6th Fleet including the Franklin D. Roosevelt, Aircraft Carrier. As this was an exercise, for safety reasons, we were required to broadcast our position before we would dive. I don't think we do that in combat because the enemy would do the same thing our destroyers did. They knew where we were and they knew what our target was.

USS Requin, underway circa 1951

They just ran to a spot between us and the carrier and waited to drop practice depth charges on us. After they killed us twice, our Captain had this great idea. We sent out our dive location, but kept running to a position ahead of the fleet before we dove. As we waited for the destroyers to pass and the carrier to come by we were rocked by explosions like in the movies. After we changed our underwear we were told that it was naval gunfire from 5 miles away. I was the first in line to get transfer papers from the yeoman. Behind me was the Captain. We later learned that it was our destroyers and real depth charges. They were practicing with live ammo as they thought we were where we said we would be. There were areas marked off that allowed live ammo. We were on one side of the line and the skimmers were on the other side. After we got our shit together, sonar called in that they had no signal.

So far this was not a good day. It gets worse. The captain told the dive officer to take us to periscope depth so we could locate the players. We hit 60 feet and the call went out "up scope." The scope went up, eyeball went to scope, another pair of fresh underwear wasted. 'Down scope, dive, dive, dive; flood all ballast tanks. Flood negative, flood safety. Bow and stern planes full down; all ahead flank; right full rudder; close all watertight doors; close all vents. Rig for collision.' Now we heard the freight train coming. We had come up in front of one big aircraft carrier.

'Trim manifold, flood all tanks from sea.' That was me! I flooded all my tanks, but I didn't think that would be much help. I braced for impact as I watched my gauges start to move. I could look around the corner and see the depth gauge. It was starting to move. Not as fast as the FDR. We hit 100 feet at the same time the carrier sounded like it was entering into the conning tower. We are at 100 feet but that is from our keel. Our periscope depth is 60 feet. How deep does a carrier sit? 40 feet? How close is the carrier? If it would miss our conning tower we would live. It passed over us. Forever!

Great. We are diving now that we don't need to dive. We pass 200 feet. 'Close all main vents, blow all main ballasts, bow and stern planes up.' We pass 300 feet. 'Blow negative, blow safety all back emergency.' Our test depth is 400 feet. We are at 500 feet. 'Trim manifold, pump all tanks to sea.' I set my valves and start my pumps. I look at my gauges and see nothing moving. I glance at the depth gauge and see we are approaching 600 feet - our crush depth. I call out, 'Too deep, request permission to go below and set pumps in series.' 'Granted!' I shut down the pumps, opened the deck hatch and drop below. I said to myself, 'I hope I know what I am doing.' I set the valves to line the pumps in series and climb up the ladder and start the pumps. I switch the valves to pump only the main trim tank and see the needle twitch. The Captain calls out, 'Send the clowns to the after room to raise the bow, then go all ahead flank.' I look but can't see the depth gauge because the dive officer is standing in front of it. It must be good, as he has started to breathe again. We all are.

All stories end well. But wait!! We start up. Up. Up. Up. 'Flood Safety, flood negative.' We will pop out of the water like a cork. But we did not. All's well. As we were going ashore in Villefranche-Sur-Mer, France, the dive officer pulled me aside and said, 'Thanks for the pumps in series, Bob, I never would have thought of that.' Most sea stories start with 'This is no shit.' I end with this: my son Pete sent away for my records 60 years later and I read this for the first time ever.

17 March 1951: Served on board the U.S.S. Requin (SSR 481) during the period 3 – 7 February 1951 during which time this vessel operated at Taranto, Italy. He contributed much toward the letter of commendation issued this vessel by Admiral M. Girosi, Commander in Chief, Italian Naval Forces, and Commander SIXTH Fleet's forwarding letter thereto. Donnelly is hereby commended for his exemplary conduct and military bearing."

J.T. Traylor, JR, LCDR, USN
EXECUTIVE OFFICER
U.S.S. REQUIN (SSR 481)

A few years before Bob was a Navy hero he served as a page boy for both Presidents Franklin Roosevelt and Harry Truman. Bob came back from the war to Pennsylvania and did this and that, and pursued his passion of flying. He bought a PT-17 and eventually based it out of Hadley Field in New Jersey. He met a daring female aviator there and after a lengthy courtship of about three weeks, they got married. They had three kids. Bob worked for a company that built the first electric car and drove it to Washington DC. He raced stock cars at tracks around PA and NJ and eventually started his own business, which he ran until he retired. Now he and Helen enjoy watching their grandkid's sporting events. Bob is writing his memoir.

Vietnam
1954 – 1975

The communist North Vietnamese had defeated the French colonials in 1954 and unified the country under communist rule. The US sent military advisors in small numbers throughout the 1950s and increased those numbers in 1961. By 1965 US combat troops were on the ground assisting and fighting with the South Vietnamese to reestablish a democratic South. From that point, for the US, the war went on for ten more years. Ground troops withdrew in 1973 and in 1975 the South fell to the communists. The exact numbers may never be known, but estimates place the cost of the war in human lives at between three and four million. The North's official numbers place the number of North Vietnamese Army and Viet Cong killed at 1.1 million. The South Vietnamese Army lost between 200,000 and 250,000 killed and the United States lost over 58,000. Numbers were a part of the war. Body counts seemed to be the measure of our success. I remember as I was growing up, every night on our little black and white TV the newscaster would report on the war and at the end of the report the channel would display in very austere and rudimentary graphics the casualty roll up for the week. The war was at times a series of intermittent skirmishes and at others it was a full up force on force brawl.

As a veteran I can't help but look back at some of the major issues of the war and note similarities to the way things evolved in both

Operations Enduring and Iraqi Freedom. Once those operations moved from something along the lines of a Major Combat Operation to sustainment and stability operations, restrictive Rules of Engagement, targeting decision authority retained at the highest echelon, and many more. One significant distinction though, which will always stick with me, is how the returning service men from the different eras were welcomed home. Again, I remember some of the images on TV showing protesters screaming at soldiers getting off buses, having just arrived from the airport, having just returned from Vietnam, screaming at them, horrible, undeserved things, throwing garbage, spitting. Whenever I came home, or greeted my troops returning home there was always a celebration and a definite sense of appreciation. And, there is a distinct difference between the Vietnam era and today in how we recognize and react to the effects of war on our warriors. Unfortunately, we're not doing much better. There are mechanism and approaches in place to help returning warriors transition back to life at home and to help them to be able to identify if they have come home with an emotional or psychological wound. As you'll see in one of the following stories, that was definitely not the case in the late '60s, early '70s in this country. Until fairly recently, Vietnam was America's longest war. During the ten years of our official involvement, millions of our men and women served in that small country. 58,000 died there. And many made it home, but didn't survive the war.

We would not have published this book without
stories from Vietnam vets.

Vet: *John*
Setting: *John sent me this chapter from his
book*
Drinks: *Leadslingers Whiskey and water (the
water was for my cat who was watching me
type)*

FIRST BLOOD:
Most of my missions during my first
couple of weeks in the battalion were pretty
forgettable; I didn't experience a lot of heavy
combat action. We were sniped at a couple of
times by some VC farmer who had a weapon
and maybe 2 or 3 rounds of ammunition in his
pockets. He might be working in a field or a rice
paddy; sometimes he even smiled and waved as
we passed by. After we had gone out of sight
Nguyen (A common Vietnamese surname that
we applied liberally to any local) would retrieve
his hidden rifle and follow after us to take a
couple of pot shots. He was generally only a
nuisance and seldom hit anyone. Once in awhile
he'd get lucky and cause a casualty. The primary
effect on us was psychological, making us feel
that we could never let our guard down nor trust
any native. Each time we were shot at we would
drop our rucks, deploy, and maneuver to get the
guy shooting at us. You just never knew how
many bad guys were out there. Sometimes we
were successful, often times as not the sniper
would quickly hide his weapon after firing his
couple of rounds and go back to tending his

paddies, smiling and waving at us as we looked for the culprit.

We also encountered a couple of booby traps, but I saw no real sustained combat. We just spent hours "humping", dealing with the incredible weight on our backs and the stupor caused by the heat, looking for signs of the bad guys and becoming increasingly bored if we didn't find much, which was a very dangerous state of mind. You naturally became less alert, less tuned in to what was going on around you, less vigilant and more lethargic from the heat. Many times these mental lapses caused by the heat and lack of action proved to be very dangerous, as inevitably this was when you would find the bad guys, or worse yet, they would find you. Many grunts will tell you that Vietnam was hours of horrible boredom sprinkled with minutes of sheer terror.

I vividly remember the first time I was engaged in a serious firefight; it was also an occasion when the Battalion Commander and his Command Sergeant Major (CSM) decided to accompany me for a day. No stress there! The BN CO was an officer whom I would come to admire greatly, and would be lucky enough to link up with again some 40 years in the future. He told me to pay no attention to him and to just do my job—I was in command. He said that he and the CSM would be happy to help out if I needed them to pull triggers; just tell them where to go and what to shoot at!

I guess that I had been in the battalion for a couple of weeks. I had been out on a couple of company-sized operations and had evidently performed pretty well in my company commander's eyes. On this occasion the company was going to work in two areas and so it was split in half. The CO took the 2nd and 3rd platoons, and gave me the mortar platoon, as infantry without their tubes, to reinforce my 1st platoon. Needless to say I was a little nervous; I would be on my own! And, as if that wasn't enough, I had not even met the Battalion Commander or the CSM before this morning, and my introduction was to be responsible for their lives in Indian country! We CA'd out of St George early in the morning and were inserted into a quiet LZ. (A CA was a helicopter borne Combat Assault into an enemy area. An LZ was a Landing Zone.) There were two types of LZ's; a cold one was unopposed by the bad guys; a hot one had the bad guys shooting at you as you came in.

Fortunately my first LZ was cold. After everyone jumped out of the birds we formed a hasty perimeter to just get a feel for the area and to lay low for a few minutes to determine if we had been detected and if any bad guys were coming to check out what had happened with the landing. We also checked to insure that there were no injuries sustained in jumping off of the birds like sprained or broken ankles, and to make sure that everyone had the equipment they needed. We then formed up into our movement formation and moved off of the LZ.

As we were moving into our assigned area of operations, we entered a densely jungled streambed where it was so dark at noon that it could have been 7 PM. The jungles in II Corps were largely triple canopy, so very little light filtered down to the jungle floor. The triple canopy was caused by trees of varying height. Mother Nature had enabled them to cope with less light in the second and third layers, and put all together the overhead was extremely thick, completely covered the area, and blocked all view of the sun and sky – kind of eerie at times. Normally it was so thick that it masked sound, making it difficult to determine the direction of the sound of small arms fire, for instance, or artillery air bursts if you were trying to triangulate your position. The triple canopy also made it impossible to pinpoint your position for friendly air support through the use of smoke grenades. You could pull the pin and throw the canister, but often times the smoke itself would drift for a long distance before it found its way up and through the entire overhanging canopy. The pilot could have no confidence in your exact location.

In most areas the underbrush was also exceedingly thick. There was an abundance of ferns, small bushes and what we called "wait a minute vines" that were somewhat like climbing rose vines in that they grew in thick tangles and were populated with an enormous number of small thorns that would lock into your jungle fatigues, web gear or even worse yet, your skin. They were horrendous, very difficult to get out of if you were snared. Plus the humidity was trapped under the layers of jungle canopy so that the trees and bushes constantly dripped moisture. It can be a distressing, creepy and scary place. In this type of area the bad guy could lie concealed only a couple of yards or even feet away and never be seen. Even if he opened fire it could be exceedingly difficult to pinpoint his location.

We were moving cautiously along the stream, hugging the banks while moving over slippery rocks interspersed with boot-sucking mud because the jungle was just too thick to move through easily or quietly. All of a sudden my point man opened up on someone he had seen ahead of us. He couldn't tell if it was VC or NVA. As the men were getting down to secure our position and I was moving up to the point we began to take fire from AK 47's from a couple of locations which indicated we had probably run into an NVA unit. This was a lot different than dealing with a local village sniper.

Shit! Here it was; my first real test and God in the form of the battalion commander was watching every move. I didn't think of anything except getting to my point man to learn what he had seen while grabbing for the radio handset to let higher know that I was in contact. My RTO and I ran in a crouch to where my point element had hit the dirt. There were rounds zipping all around us, this is the first time I realized that the bad guys used green tracers as opposed to our red ones. They just seemed to float . . . Some made strange cracking noises, which I eventually learned was caused by their going by close to my ear. My heart was thudding and I was breathing in gasps due to the exertion in that incredibly humid air and the fear; to say nothing of the adrenaline pouring into my system; the sweat was pouring down my face making it hard to see.

I suddenly knew that I had a guy shot because I heard the scream for "Medic!!" Oh shit, my heartbeat tripled instantly; that is one of the most horrible cries for an infantry commander to hear because it means one of your soldiers has been hit. I ran over to find one of my guys bleeding profusely from an arm wound that proved to be not too serious; the cloying, kinda coppery smell of fresh blood— my first introduction. My medic had the situation well in hand.

The firing eventually stopped. We made a hasty check of the area, found no enemy bodies but a couple of blood trails that indicated that some of them had been hit. We reformed and continued cautiously up the stream for another hour or more until we saw a waterfall that looked to be about 30 feet high in the distance. As we moved forward, the stream banks got higher and steeper. Eventually we got close to the falls, so I ordered a halt; we'd take a break for lunch on the riverbanks. While still incredibly humid, the air was cooler here thanks to the mist generated when the water coming over the falls crashed into the stream below.

Because I didn't want to be caught by surprise I decided that I needed a presence on the high ground above the falls. I led one of my squads with a gun (M60 machine gun) team on a climb beside the falls until we reached the top to act as an OP or observation post. The going was tough as the bank was steep and the underbrush exceedingly thick. In some cases we pulled ourselves up by grasping at roots or rock outcroppings, hoping we wouldn't lose our grip and fall. When we reached the top we were soaked with sweat and totally out of breath.

After we had caught our breath the squad leader and I selected a good position that would ensure security, so I went back down to the rest of the two platoons that were under my command. They had moved into the jungle on either side of the stream so as to not be visible to anyone on the high ground. They shook off their rucksacks and dug into them for some cans of C's. Several of the guys refilled their canteens from the cold, clear stream. I needed some time to think about what we were going to do next; climb the bank and continue our hump, or backtrack to where the slope wasn't as high or steep and we'd be less vulnerable during the climb. There was a good chance that our earlier firefight had alerted a larger NVA unit of our presence.

As we were taking the break a couple of the guys were exploring the falls and discovered a cave entrance behind the water. I got a squad together and we climbed up to investigate. As we entered the mouth of the cave it became obvious that we had uncovered a fully stocked NVA hospital. There were several rooms, which included a surgical suite and a couple of wards with bamboo beds. There were some bloody bandages piled in the corner of one room that looked fairly fresh. There was also a good supply of medical gear as well as assorted cooking pans in a kitchen area that had a vent that went up to the surface.

We also discovered a couple of foot locker-type boxes in what appeared to be a storeroom that we carried outside to investigate. We opened one and found that it contained, among other things, several lacy black bras and panties. So there were either nurses present or this place also served as a "comfort station" for war-weary NVA troops. Needless to say my guys got pretty excited about this find, wanting a bra or pair of panties as a unique souvenir. I presented the Battalion Commander with a pair of the panties as a souvenir; forty years later he still had them! It was quite possible that the NVA that we had encountered earlier was a guard or care-taking force for this hospital.

As we were admiring our find of lingerie and letting our imagination run wild, all of a sudden all hell broke loose on top of the falls. I could hear M16s and my M60, also AK 47s and RPGs going off. I grabbed my weapon and ammo, told the closest guys to follow me, and started up the cliff side. I yelled at my platoon sergeant to get the rest of the guys into good secure and concealed positions, and to be prepared to reinforce me should I call for him. I cannot adequately describe the feeling of urgency and the "rush" that comes at such a time. When I got to the top my lungs were bursting and I couldn't see from all of the sweat streaming down my face. All I wanted to do was stop, but my guys were in contact. We collected ourselves and moved forward cautiously, but quickly.

All of a sudden I saw my M60 gunner, a tall, strapping guy, standing buck-assed naked in the middle of the stream firing furiously while screaming for more ammo. His ammo bearer was hiding behind a big rock, too scared to move forward to resupply his gunner. I moved up beside him, smacked him in the helmet with the butt of my CAR 15, and screamed at him to

"MOVE!" as I pointed to his gunner who was running for the bank and swearing furiously at his ammo bearer to get that "goddamn ammo up here!!" The little guy took off like a scared rabbit and helped the gunner furiously load the gun so that he could get back into the fight.

I took the rest of the guys I'd run up the hill with on a flanking movement around where I determined most of the enemy fire was originating. The adrenaline was rushing; there was incredible noise and the sharp smell of gunpowder that hung close to the ground under the jungle canopy that burned my eyes as much as the sweat that was pouring into them. I was breathing so hard I could hardly talk. I could hear the thunder of my heart in my ears; my eyes were watering and my thought was that I needed to do whatever was required to make sure that I didn't lose anyone. I could see fleeting figures in the dense underbrush, men in khaki wearing pith helmets. During that mad dash I took my first aimed shot at another human being, an NVA soldier scanning the underbrush and looking for a target, and he went down; his head exploding in a red mist. I don't remember any emotional reaction but immense satisfaction; my first kill. I can still see that guy as though it were only yesterday.

Our fire was too great and the enemy disappeared into the jungle, dragging any dead and wounded with them. That was one of the frustrating things about this war; the bad guys normally took their casualties with them so that you couldn't have the satisfaction of seeing dead ones. Often the best you could find was the ubiquitous blood trail left as dead and wounded soldiers were dragged away, or spilled by walking wounded as they made their escape. No satisfaction; kinda like the title of a popular song by the Rolling Stones, *Satisfaction,* that often played in the Weapons Room in the gym at West Point when we went for a hamburger and shake: *"I can't get no . . . satisfaction".* I looked for but couldn't find the body of the NVA soldier that I knew I had shot.

After the contact was over I called my security team together to find out what had happened and why my machine gunner was completely naked while on guard! It turned out that several of my guys had been taking advantage of the cold and clear stream to get cleaned up when the NVA approached. They had literally been caught with their pants down; kind of embarrassing for a seasoned US combat infantryman. Even still, they had seen the NVA first before being detected. The NVA soldiers were obviously not expecting to encounter any Americans, as they were moving in a loose formation with their weapons on their shoulders or being carried loosely at their sides. The enemy soldiers were probably returning to the hospital cave for the night. They were talking, joking and laughing which allowed my guys to get the drop on them even though they were in a very compromising position! That could explain why I suffered no casualties; we luckily caught the NVA totally by surprise and their return fire was hasty and ineffective.

As things quieted down I grabbed my squad leader and furiously chewed his ass. I was angry but awfully relieved when all of my guys were present and accounted for with no holes in their bodies. How could he have let his guys be caught in such a compromising position? Didn't he realize that there were possibly enemy soldiers in the area, especially after our earlier firefight?

He was really embarrassed as he was one of the oldest guys in the unit in regards to time in country and in combat; he was one of the most experienced. After I finished yelling at him he promised to never ever again get naked in Indian Country! I told him to secure the area again as the rest of us would soon climb up to join him and continue our mission and try to track the guys we had just fought with. After I rejoined the rest of my unit at the foot of the falls the reaction set in. During the contact and dressing down afterwards I remember being scared, and incredibly pissed off at the bad guys for screwing with us while I had the BN Commander in my formation, and at my guys for being so stupid. As I sat down to take a break and get my breathing under control my hands started to shake and I couldn't light a cigarette. I tried to hide the shaking and it took a while before it disappeared. There was no way I could take a much-needed drink from my canteen!

We had a "thing" about the NVA—they were kinda regarded as supermen by most American grunts in the area. The Viet Cong, or VC, both local and main force, were primarily local farmers, not usually heavily armed, although some of their units were pretty good. This was particularly true of the "Main Force VC" as opposed to the local guerrilla groups. The main force guys were in organized units, much better equipped and trained than the real local guys, but still no match for a US unit. They had their designated areas of responsibility and did not go back to their villages at night.

The NVA, on the other hand, were well trained (we thought) and outfitted regular troops, much better equipped and much more aggressive. The VC would usually melt away after firing a few shots, or a B40 rocket or two; the NVA regulars would usually stand and fight if you were in a smaller than company sized unit. They had learned from experience that they were usually no match for a full American infantry company with all of its organic firepower and access to formidable support like artillery, armed Army helicopters and jets from the Air Force or Navy. They were certainly not supermen in my experience, but you could generally expect a pretty good fight if you crossed their path.

The rest of the mission was pretty quiet. We moved up the cliff side by the falls and cautiously followed a couple of the blood trails. The BN Commander and CSM left us when we found a suitable PZ for his bird. When the blood trails petered out we patrolled the general area for another day, hoping to regain contact with the NVA we had chased from the falls. While we periodically saw signs of their presence we never again re-established contact with them. After 2 or 3 days we were airlifted back to St. George. The final toll for the operation was one US wounded, and, we suspected, several NVA killed or wounded, even though we never found a body.

The BN Commander, Dragon 6 (The 14th Infantry was known as the Golden

Dragons), as I said, was a guy who I really respected. He was every inch the Regular Army officer and commander. LTC Victor M. Robertson Jr. was from South Carolina and was a graduate of The Citadel. One day, as I passed his hooch (a tent called a GP Small or General Purpose Small) on St George one day shortly after the hospital cave fight, he stopped me and asked me to come in. Aw shit, what had I done now? Why would the BN Commander want to talk with me, a mere lieutenant, in his hooch? Had I screwed up royally on that mission in the stream? I got even more scared when he told me to sit down and offered me a scotch. We talked for a few minutes about my experiences up to that time, and what I thought of my initial time in the battalion, and then I found out why the good treatment. He asked if I would be willing to take over Fox Force, the Battalion recon platoon. I was shocked, and my initial reaction was "no fucking way"... to myself of course.

The recon platoon is without a doubt the choice combat assignment for any infantry lieutenant. But this was different. This WAS combat and Fox had quite a reputation, a bunch of tough guys who got into a contact with the bad guys every time they went out. They wore bright red scarves, even in the field, and were currently being led by a muscular, intimidating staff sergeant or E6, Jimmy Harris from Mississippi. I had personally witnessed him coming into the chow tent on St George. He'd get his food, and when he chose a place to sit everyone else moved away. Scared shitless!! I wasn't sure that I was enough of a combat veteran to take on this job. Dragon 6 told me I could think about it for a while and I was one happy "el tee" to escape the Dragon's Lair.

I screwed up and walked by the Old Man's hooch a few days later after another mission that included a couple of firefights; was once again invited inside and we talked over another bottle of scotch, Johnny Walker Red as I remember. The boss was pretty persuasive this time and "asked" directly that I accept the job. I finally agreed to become Fox 6. The recon platoon is THE plum assignment for an infantry LT, but I wasn't sure that I could deal with these Fox guys. I was really apprehensive and unsure if I was ready for command of this type of unit.

I was now a legitimate combat infantryman, having been given the coveted CIB (Combat Infantryman's Badge) by the BN Command Sergeant Major. He was a great guy and wanted me to have his original CIB that was issued to him during the Korean War. Unlike the modern ones made from a piece of stamped metal, this was made of sterling silver. It was the only one that I wore for the rest of my military career.

The Fox guys were special; the whole BN looked at them with a certain amount of fear, a lot of respect, and even more awe. Other guys in the chow line would stand aside and let the recon guys go first if they showed up to eat. Anyone stupid enough to go into the jungle wearing a bright red scarf . . . But, this started one of the most enduring sets of male relationships that I would ever have. The camaraderie of men who have shared close combat together is like no other imaginable.

As I was preparing to take over Fox, I did some serious thinking. I was certainly a little apprehensive about taking command of the most aggressive unit in the battalion; I wondered if I was up to it. But I found that I had a growing inner confidence; I was now an experienced combat infantry lieutenant. I had been shot at, and had not failed my men, or myself. My company commander had enough faith in my abilities to give me half of the company to command, in my own AO, on a couple of missions. I had seen men killed and wounded, and I had killed as well. I believe that West Point had prepared me well for the requirements of combat command. The four-year "system" had placed a lot of stress on us in many ways, weeding out a lot of guys who couldn't handle the challenge, and developing those who could. I had been challenged and had persevered. The system had provided the basics; the rest was up to each individual graduate.

By this time some of the wetness behind my ears had dried, and I had become comfortable with my responsibility for men's lives. I had trained for years to be a combat leader and finally really was one. I found that I enjoyed the feeling of command, that I was pretty good at the basics, and that there was a sense of fulfillment to be doing that for which I had trained. In reality, I was really enjoying myself!

While I had been in the battalion only a little more than a month, and still had my greatest tests ahead of me, deep down I was pretty confident that I could handle Fox— and hopefully do it well. I believe that I took command of Fox sometime in early August.

John served for twenty-four years as an infantry officer in the US Army, including a prestigious company command tour in The Old Guard, 1st Battalion, 3rd Infantry in Washington DC. Among other high visibility assignments, through a highly competitive process, John was selected as a Foreign Area Officer, Japan Specialist and served in Japan as a liaison to the senior Japanese Military Headquarters in Tokyo. John retired from the Army and worked for Raytheon back in Japan on the Patriot Missile program. He continued to serve in this civilian position and was responsible for the deployment of technical advisors in support of Operation Desert Storm. After several more years in Japan he returned to the States continuing to work in the private sector. He remains involved in veteran support organizations.

John was awarded the Silver Star, the Bronze Star with Valor Device and two oak leaf clusters, the Army Commendation Medal with Valor Device and one oak leaf cluster, and the Combat Infantryman's Badge.

As John put his experience in Vietnam, "It did cause me to grow up quickly, taught me that the heaviest responsibility imaginable was that of being responsible for other men's' lives in a combat environment. I also came to really respect, honor and appreciate anyone who has served this country. "

****

Vet: *Don*
Setting: *Don allowed me to print this chapter from his memoir*
Drinks: *Shot(s) of Avion tequila and a couple of Coronas for me.*

SPLUSH!
A chapter in *Farm Boy to Fly Boy*,
the memoirs of Captain Donald A. "Sabre" Baker, USN(RET)

The day of September 8, 1967 started like most any of the previous days of combat operations flying from the aircraft carrier USS Oriskany (CVA 34) in the Gulf of Tonkin during the Vietnam War. However, for me, it didn't turn out like all the previous days operating from Yankee Station. Yankee Station is what the Navy called the carrier operating area off the coast of North Vietnam, close to the 38th parallel on the map. There was also Dixie Station, which was off the coast of Northern South Vietnam. Our air wing operating tempo, OPTEMPO as it was called, had moved from major "Alfa" strikes of twenty to thirty aircraft down to small flights of six to eight aircraft composed of four to six attack aircraft, accompanied by two fighter aircraft. The task of the attack aircraft was to drop bombs and fire rockets at ground targets identified for the specific mission. The fighter aircraft were to protect the attack aircraft from enemy fighters. This shift in OPTEMPO was a welcome relief from the previous Alfa-strike operations in which we often flew into the teeth of enemy anti-aircraft fire from their Surface to Air Missiles (SAMS) and/or 57-millimeter anti-aircraft guns.

The flight schedule for that day had me and my wingman, Al Aston, flying escort for a flight of four Skyhawk (A4D) attack aircraft on a mission to a target area in the Northeast sector of North Vietnam, just a few miles from the border of China. The attack squadron flight leader briefed us, prior to the mission, what the primary target was and, also specified an alternate target in the event the weather prohibited attacking the primary target. We were to rendezvous the flight directly above, or "overhead," the aircraft carrier and proceed as a coordinated group to the target.

I was catapulted of the carrier deck in an assigned Crusader (F8C) and preceded to a rendezvous position directly above the location of the aircraft carrier. As I awaited the arrival of my wingman I was told he would not be launching due to mechanical problems with his assigned aircraft. I immediately looked for the attack group and found they were already proceeding to the target area. I tried to join them as quickly as possible to be with them before they arrived at the coast of North Vietnam. As I approached the coast I heard the typical communications of aircraft on such a raid. I crossed the coast, becoming "feet dry," a term meaning flying over land.

I saw the primary target ahead, but could not see the attack aircraft anywhere in the vicinity. I called the flight leader and asked where he was; he replied the flight was over the target. I told him I was in the vicinity of the target but did not have the flight in sight. He then told me the flight was attacking the alternate target. Wow! What a surprise! It was clear to me I needed to get the hell out of there as quickly as possible. I immediately headed South toward the gulf to get "feet wet" quickly to avoid possibly engaging enemy aircraft. The attack group, after completing their mission, proceeded back to the ship without me seeing them at any time.

As I was crossing the North Vietnamese coast heading South, I searched for a target of opportunity I might hit with the 5-inch rockets. We were seldom loaded with 5-inch rockets, but this particular mission specified the unusual arms load. Normally the F8C Crusader was loaded with the heat seeking air-to-air Sidewinder (AIM-9D) missiles, an excellent weapon designed to shoot down enemy planes. I had the-5 inch rockets and Sidewinders too, but I wanted to find a suitable target for the rockets. I spotted what appeared to be a radar site on the coast of Dollar Island, as we called a small island near the coast of North Vietnam.

I armed the rockets and rolled into a dive, lined up the target in my site as I dove from about ten thousand feet altitude. Shortly after I fired the rockets, as I was pulling up off the target, I heard a loud thump and a jolt that shook the airplane. Apparently the North Vietnamese radar site had a AAA battery nearby that fired at my airplane as I crossed over the area. I continued to head south over water while climbing to above ten thousand feet altitude. The aircraft had lost all electrical power, but still responded to the flight controls and the engine continued running. Without proper electrical power the aircraft navigation instruments and radios would not function. I thought I had an alternative electrical supply because the Crusader was equipped with a deployable emergency electrical generator: a ram air turbine or RAT. I pulled the handle to deploy the RAT, but to my disappointment the electrical power was not restored by the RAT...the "dirty rat."

Well, here I was without navigation aids and without a radio to let the ship know my situation. The loss of the radio was not an immediate problem, but added difficulty to my circumstances later. Good weather favored my return to the vicinity of the aircraft carrier since I could navigate visually without complication of clouds or haze diminishing visibility. The most pressing problem was, without electrical power, the trim tab control on the flight control stick was not functioning, leaving me with excessive pressure on the control stick to maintain level flight. As I continued on my return to the ship, with the plane seeming to lose power, I judged I might need to eject from the aircraft. Therefore, I removed my kneepad from my left leg to ensure the metal instrument would not interfere with an ejection, nor become an object of injury. Additionally, since there was excessive pressure required to move the flight control stick, I knew I would not be able to eject using the normal method of raising both hands above my head to pull down on the face curtain. Therefore, I reached down below my legs just loosening the alternate ejection seat firing handle to make sure it would not bind when trying to pull it up, should I need to eject.

With the ship in sight I started planning to make an approach for landing. Of concern at this point was the total amount of fuel remaining. The arresting cable, we called it the wire, would be set for the normal landing weight of my aircraft. If my aircraft weight was above the expected weight the arresting wire could break. Such a situation would be catastrophic to the men and equipment on the deck. Not knowing exactly how much fuel I had, but suspecting that the duration of the flight left me with an excess, I decided to make the plane lighter as well as attract the attention of the ship. I continued descending, maneuvering to clear an area to the port side of the ship in an attempt to eject the Sidewinders as unguided rockets with the emergency switch designed for such a contingency. Surprisingly, without normal electrical power the missiles ejected from the rails and splashed in the water visible from the ship. Interestingly, my assigned wingman, Al, was on the Landing Signal Officer (LSO) platform near the landing area. Al told me later he saw the missiles hit the water. He said his thought at the time was somebody's going to be in big trouble with the ship's captain and the Air Wing Commander by launching something into the water so close to the ship.

I hoped someone on the ship would see the missile splashes and tell the Air Boss in the control tower to keep me in sight, however, it didn't happen, compounding my problems in the latter stages of my approach. I continued in a descent to line up astern of the ship for a straight-in approach. I picked up visual sight of the meatball, which is the primary aide to keep on the proper glide path for landing. The meat mall is a light projected out in space from the landing area and is the primary aid for the pilot to land safely. Once the meatball is in sight, the pilot keeps it centered between a set of datum lights to stay on the proper glide slope to land in the optimum location in the landing area. With the meatball centered the tail hook of the aircraft should engage the third, or number three wire, of the four wires on deck.

With the meatball in sight I continued a straight-in approach on the glide path. The straight-in-approach was normally interpreted by the Air Boss that the aircraft has no radio and may have mechanical problems. I lowered the landing gear and the tail hook, noting in this condition, the aircraft did not have enough power to maintain level flight, but had sufficient power to keep on the proper glide slope. As I got closer to the ship, an A4D Skyhawk flew in front of me while making a turning approach to the landing area. The A4D was only a couple hundred feet in front of me, so I adjusted my flight path to be slightly below his, but to be as close as possible to the proper glide path. We continued down the glide path together when the A4D received a wave off signal and leveled out to fly past the ship. I was relieved to see I could proceed unabated to make my landing. However, it seems things don't always work out just like one might like. This was one of those times! Remember, the arresting wires are supposed to be set for the weight of the aircraft, and, in this case, the setting had to be changed from the A4D to the much heavier setting of the F8C. Because I was so close to the A4, in fact just slightly below his jet wash, there was not an adequate amount of time to re-set for the weight of my aircraft. I was very close to the ship at this point when given a Wave Off. The wave-off was signaled to me by the Landing Signal Officer (LSO) flashing the wave-off Lights on a panel near the meatball. The wave off is a mandatory signal and must be responded to without question, as a matter of safety. I pushed the throttle forward for full power but the engine response was not adequate to clear the landing area. The aircraft touched down in the landing area just past all the wires.

Now, here I was following a Bolter, which is a touchdown in the landing area without catching any of the wires; so I added power to go around for another try. Yep, I was on a Bolter and trying to climb out to an altitude of 1000 feet to attempt another pass. I still had to maneuver around the jet wash of the A4D in front of me while making a gentle climbing turn to the downwind leg. The A4D, by the way, didn't have radios either. I was able to turn the aircraft downwind but could only reach an altitude of 500 feet. As I looked at the ship from abeam, I evaluated my chances of intercepting the glide slope to make an approach from this low altitude. Another however! Although I had the throttle fully forward to full power, the aircraft was losing airspeed as I tried to maintain level flight. It was essential to maintain the minimum altitude of 500 feet, but the airspeed continued to deteriorate to the point when I felt the slight shudder sensation of a pre-stall. This was my signal that I could no longer stay with the plane in an attempt to land on the ship.

Holding the stick with my right hand, remember I couldn't trim out the force on the stick to keep it from nosing over; I pulled the alternate firing handle with my left hand initiating the ejection sequence. As the seat fired, I remember seeing the empty cockpit with the long ejection seat barrel extending above the cockpit and seeing the plane nosing over rapidly. I tumbled slightly in the air and looked up to see the parachute had opened successfully. My thought was, "wow that worked, what do I do next...oh yeah, deploy the seat pan." Underneath the seat pan was a life raft with various survival gear, which, once released by pulling a small handle on the left side of the seat, would drop down about six to eight feet on a lanyard. As I reached for the handle, I looked down saying to myself "too late." *Splush*!!

This is where the wonderful training of the Navy paid off. All of us Naval Aviators who flew from aircraft carriers trained for possible ejection by joining the "Oh My Ass Club." The club was joined by pulling a face curtain to be fired up a railing about 15 feet on a simulated ejection seat. With my ejection from the aircraft the following actions took little conscious thought. As I entered the water, I continued to reach for the handle, deploying the seat pan with my left hand. I then used both hands to simultaneously remove the quick release fittings on my harness. As I surfaced, I threw the fittings away from me, leaving me clear of the parachute. I don't remember pulling the toggles on the Mae West to inflate it, but I must have because I was floating just fine with my head above water. I checked the lanyard to the seat pan, it was still attached satisfactorily. I do remember there was a lot of jet fuel in water where I landed. Apparently I was very close to where the plane hit the water. The water wasn't noticeably cold and the waves were not very high providing little trouble in the water.

Now I thought somebody would come pick me up...for surely they saw me eject from the plane. I was right; as I looked around I saw a large bow wake in front of the plane guard destroyer. During all carrier operations a plane guard destroyer was always on station nearby with the duty of picking up downed airmen, as necessary. Additionally, we always had a helicopter airborne tasked with the same mission. Seeing the bow wake and smoke pouring from the stack of the plane guard destroyer pointed straight at me, I said to myself, "*come on helo!*" Part of my concern was I had a friend who was sucked into the intakes of a destroyer trying to rescue him...so I was hoping for the Helo. Sure enough, the Helo beat the destroyer to the scene above me. Immediately dropping a swimmer in the water next to me, he checked to see if I was free of the parachute. The Helo hoisted me and the swimmer into the copter and we proceeded to the flight deck of the carrier.

I stepped out of the Helo, declined the corpsman's offer to put me in a stretcher and was greeted by the Carrier Air Wing Commander (CAG) himself. One of the corpsmen escorted me down a few ladders to Sickbay. I was later admonished for not getting in one of those wire stretchers on board ship, but I had seen them maneuvering down those steep ladders with others and decided," *not for me!*" In sickbay I was treated for a small laceration, but otherwise suffered no other apparent problems and was back flying the very next day. In those days we didn't have cell phones, WIFI or email, but I was permitted to get a two-line telegraph note off to my wife telling her I had ejected and was okay, so she could ignore any false rumors that might circulate back home, as was sometimes prone to occur.

Following his time with the "Sundowners" of Fighter Squadron 111, when he was shot down, Don did a tour as Commanding Officer of Fighter Squadron 41, the "Black Aces," followed by a tour as the Commanding Officer of the USS Milwaukee, AOR 2, a replenishment oilier. He was also the Executive Officer of the aircraft carrier America. Don continued his illustrious career and served as a "Commodore" in command of 11 Mobile Logistics Support Force ships and finally was the Current Operations Officer, "J3", serving in the Command Center of Commander Naval Forces Atlantic until he retired as a Captain after 30 years of service in the US Navy. I met Don in the same veteran's writing group I met Joe B. Don's a great guy with a great career and a great story.

****

Vet: *Clyde*
Setting: *Clyde and I talked over the phone*
Drinks: *None*

Story: "We were on an operation with a company of American grunts. We were sitting as a blocking force. There were two tanks and we had a lieutenant with us but he was new in country so he let me run the show. We went out on this blocking force for a bigger operation and we see nothing and we're sitting there for hours. We expected to spend the night there. We figured we be eating cold C-rations and sleeping on the ground next to the tank. All of sudden we get a call to come back in, so we're all happy man. We're going back to cold beer, cots and an no-kidding warm meal, so we're actually happy. I asked the grunt lieutenant if he wanted his guys to ride on the tank. He said, 'Sure.' I remember telling him to make sure his guys put their feet above the fender. I told him something else, but I really don't remember. He never passed that on to his guys. So, we're heading back in, I'm sitting on the tank commander's hatch on top of the tank on the right side. I was sitting there, I was so comfortable, it was a nice warm day, I was so relaxed; everything was going great. All of a sudden I remember taking a deep breath of air and the air was hot, it was really hot. I started getting dizzy, and I thought to myself, uh oh, this is it. The next thing I remember, my life is like a brown blob.

I don't know how to explain it, but that's how my life seemed to me at the time, I was just a brown blob, I wasn't living, I wasn't dead. I started to talk to myself, I said, 'Man, you gotta snap out of this, you've got to come back to life, you can't do this, you've got to come back to life.' It seemed to me that I talked to myself for about twenty minutes, now how long it actually went on I don't know. Soon, I saw a little bit of light and it reminded me of like when you drink a glass of water and you look through the bottom of the glass; it was all distorted. It took quite a while, it seemed to me, to start functioning and everything. I remember standing up and looking around and there were wounded grunts lying all over the place. I didn't know what the hell happened. I saw people's mouths moving, but I couldn't hear a word. It took me a long time to realize we hit a damn mine.

What amazed me was that I never heard the explosion. Finally, I started to function. I was almost in a daze, useless, I should have jumped down and started helping with the wounded, but instead I just stood there trying to figure out what the hell happened. I felt like I was in a daze for two weeks after that. Before that I was getting promoted so damn fast I didn't even want the damn promotions, I wasn't ready for them. After that, that changed my life, because all of a sudden I started second guessing myself, I had trouble making decisions. When I saw people, when I saw two or three people talking I thought, they're talking about me. I was not the same person, I didn't trust anybody anymore, I got such a temper, I didn't understand what this was all about. I mean that's the way it was. The tank was lying in a hole three feet deep and five foot round. The whole right front side of the tank was in that hole. It had blown off three road wheels in the front. Same side I was sitting on. Our company commander came out with maintenance and he felt this was all mine and the lieutenant's fault. I felt sorry for the lieutenant, it wasn't my decision it was the grunt lieutenant's that directed we go through there. My company commander blamed me for this and I had to live with this. I don't know how many people lost legs or even died from that incident, you know? Then they gave me orders for drill instructor school and I knew I couldn't do that because I couldn't remember, like a drunk in a bunk, I couldn't remember how it was supposed to be laid out. I couldn't remember none of that stuff, so I knew I couldn't make it through drill instructor school. So, I opted to get out of the Marine Corps. When I got out, as you well know, that was the worst period of my life, because everybody looked down upon us. I came home and I had no job, no family, no girlfriend. I was so damned depressed all the time. Like most Vietnam vets, I contemplated suicide. I even thought about how I would do it. I thought how this life isn't worth living; it's not worth the effort. The only thing that prevented me from committing suicide was that I believe God put us here for a reason. I think we need to fulfill that reason. I was more comfortable in the war in Vietnam than I was in this country. We had no support groups back then. They have plenty of support now, which is good, but back then we didn't know about post-traumatic stress. I had it, but I didn't know nothing about it. It was a very difficult time for me, very difficult. We didn't even talk to each other about it, we didn't want to talk about the war and we didn't even want to hear about the military. We didn't even want to talk about it."

Clyde, with black tee shirt

Clyde told me three great stories. This volume will have one and the other two will come out in future volumes. I've included this particular story, because although it was told about an incident that occurred a half century ago, it continues for Clyde to this day. As you read in his own words, Clyde struggled with the after effects of his injuries and there wasn't a clear path to take back then to get help. After Vietnam Clyde worked as a bricklayer and in printing. His biggest challenge was living with undiagnosed PTSD (Post Traumatic Stress Disorder) and TBI (Traumatic Brain Injury). He had to work four times harder to get the same things done as others. He couldn't think of the simplest things, like remembering to put the car in reverse, one he'd driven for years. He had a tough time getting along with people and crowds bothered him. And as he put it, "I drank way too much, that was the only time I felt relaxed." For 40 years he didn't know his issues were from PTSD and TBI. TBI wasn't even an identified condition until recently. Clyde struggled with finding life worth living, the only thing that saved him was the belief that God put him here for a reason; he couldn't quit without fulfilling that reason.

But it was difficult. His family life suffered, he suffered. In a reflection of his character Clyde believed that he had these experiences and these difficulties so that he could be there to help others deal with and work through the same issues. Others view him as an example and a role model; if he can live through all of what he went through, maybe they could too. Clyde finds reward in writing and has written seven books. His greatest satisfaction is when someone tells him they've directly benefitted from reading one of his books. A man came up to him and told him he read his book, "God Help Me," and finally understood what his daughter, who had TBI, was going through.

Clyde has also used his experience to create organizations and efforts to help prevent veteran suicides. You can find more of Clyde's stories in future volumes of "There I was..." and the soon to be re-released book of Clyde's; "Tracks."

Panama
20 December 1989 – 31 January 1990

Issues between the United States and Panama had escalated contributing to President Bush's decision to invade in late 1989. A Marine had been killed and President Noriega and his Panamanian Defense Forces were a threat to the approximately 35,000 Americans living there at the time. Noriega was also believed to be responsible for contributing to the drug trafficking through Panama. The war on drugs in America, declared by President Nixon in 1971, was in full swing in 1989. The US was also aware of the human rights abuses in Panama, enabled by Noriega and the PDF and they also interpreted his actions to be a threat to the neutrality of the Panama Canal and thus a violation of the Torrijos–Carter Treaties. The decision was made and Operation Just Cause went into action. The force included numerous units including the 82d Airborne Division, 75th Ranger Regiment, 7th Infantry Division, elements of the 5th Infantry Division and many more. The operation included over 300 aircraft and saw the first combat employment of the F-117 Nighthawk. Guillermo Endara was sworn in as the new president and Manuel Noriega eventually surrendered on 3 January 1990 and was flown to the US. The fighting went on for a few weeks, ending on 31 January 1990.

Vet: *"LA"*

Setting: *LA is driving back from a week at Fort Bragg supporting an exercise. I've just gotten home from the same event. We hadn't had a chance to talk while there so we figured while he was driving we'd capture his story.*

Drinks: *I was drinking; hopefully LA was not. I was having a Leadslingers Whiskey and club soda.*

Story: LA prefaced his story with a qualification, he said, "This is more of a philosophy thing; in a way, what you are doing is fantastic, (capturing vet stories) but it fits in with my career narrative very well. My career narrative basically is, I have personally been around a lot of heroes, around a lot of people who've done amazing things. I've actually watched them, been real close to them, the distinction I made to many audiences, please don't mistake that, being close to someone, being close to a hero; don't mistake that for being a hero myself. Because, I can tell you really and truly, I've been close to a lot of things, I've never done any fucking hero shit, ever, like ever, and I mean like ever. That doesn't mean I don't have stories to tell about other people, or that I don't have events that sound really great, they do, but they're not really hero stories, they're really not. They're just not hero stories."

LA continues, "Okay, so the untold stories from Panama, actually Panama was actually really short. It was kinda like one big mission, not like a combat deployment per se, because we launched in for the invasion of

Panama and within, you know, seven days, we're back home. That's really short, so I never really calculated that as a combat deployment. But, a lot of neat things happened.

When we were going to do Panama, we had a Joint exercise, Special Ops oriented. We had a series of Joint Special Operations exercises before Panama, because, the National Command Authority had considered, what happens if Noriega continues to get bad and worse than bad. So, the President and the National Command Authority had already put a lot of important things into place. That was the Bush administration, Bush number one and secretary Cheney. The commander of US Southern Command and the commander of US Special Operations Command and the XVIII Corps commander were all pretty close. There was one US Southern Command commander who got fired, because he never did or considered doing anything about Noriega. The new Southern Command commander had been a different character, and that was General Thurman. So, as soon as that high level command shuffle took place we went through a series of exercises called Blue Spoon. They were practicing airfield seizures and airborne insertions, basically rehearsals to take over the country. These were built around primarily special operations forces with some conventional forces in support; submarines, the 7th Infantry out of Fort Ord, in California. They were going to be the follow on forces. The initial forces were going to all be special operations. So, us, the XVIII Airborne Corps portion of the plan, the Corps staff and the 82d would seize Torrijos Tocumen.

So, we're going to take two airfields, Rio Hado and Torrijos Tocumen. Very significant planning went into the very first combat deployment of the F-117, and the targets for the F-117 were Rio Hado, a barracks of a battalion of 2000 soldiers, I think, Panamanian Defense Forces. There was a great fighter pilot who ran that, General Feast, but that was the first deployment of the F-117. You could actually see the explosions out the door of the C-130s, you could see the two explosions. So, the purpose of my unit, was not only to deploy with the Army Rangers, but we were to provide battle damage assessment for those 117s back to 12th Air Force, the combat NAF for US Southern Command. And to get that BDA, I was basically the Airman for the 75th Ranger Regiment. And we did a lot of great things. I jumped right in with the Regimental Commander, I preceded him. I was on the first C-130. But, the first Airman out of the first C-130 was a Staff Sergeant Chet Heedwin; he was a bike chaser. The tactic we had was the combat controllers would push out a motorcycle and, in this case, it was a mini-bike. They had their own chutes, so they'd push out the bike and then the Airman would jump out after it and chase the bike in the air, so, wherever the bike landed, the bike chaser would land, de-rig the bike, get on it and then race to the runway and start clearing it, because we had a follow on about 20 to 25 minutes after. So, Chet Heedwin was actually shot when he jumped out. So, you're under canopy, which is arguably high risk, but he was shot, but he didn't tell anyone. He didn't say anything and I was unaware he'd been shot. Just goes to show what kind of a guy he was, what kind of a hero, even though he sustained that injury, he cleared that runway within twenty minutes so the air-land mission could come in. One of the MC-130 that would do the first air-land lost an engine. Then we had to worry about a three engine takeoff, which is was actually a big deal and we had to go back to a higher command authority to get permission for the 130 to take off with three versus four engines. So, you had Air Force combat controllers, Air Force Pararescuemen, Air Force TACP, and you had an ALO all assigned to the 75th Ranger Regiment. It's amazing that I ever become an officer in the TACP business, because I basically, when the Rangers needed close air support, I preferred to get that from an AH-6 Little Bird, or an AC-130 Gunship. I became quite aggravated when the ALO called in an A-37, and had to tell the ALO to get him out of the way, because he was just going to get in the way and wasn't going to be very useful for this particular fight. So, it's a wonder I ever got into the TACP business. I told the ALO to basically shut the fuck up, stay off the net, stay out of my way. Because, if you think about it, basically it was an airfield, so unlike just the maneuver units maneuvering around on the battlefield where close air support, you didn't care where you got it from, but with the complexity of an airfield seizure, is that you've got all kinds of aircraft coming into that airfield. You still need close air support, I'm not arguing that, but the complexity of it is better if you're an air traffic controller at the airfield, to mix and manage all those assets, from airlift, to close air support, it's just better if you have that kind of perspective, a more holistic way, which is the air traffic control versus a forward air control sense. The ALO's only going to talk to the A-37 and not really provide any substantial deconfliction, then we've really got problems. We have a lot of airplanes doing a lot of different things around that airfield; it's a whole different level of complexity. I was holding 130's out, not letting them land, I had helicopters transiting, Little Birds, literally fifteen feet above our heads doing things, I've got an AC-130 gunship overhead, so, having an A-37, gave me no real additional firepower that we needed. So, basically it wasn't a big job for the ALO. So, I told the ALO to shut up and the Regimental commander, at the time was Col Kiernan, who would later become Gen Kiernan, said, 'Mike, if it's air, you've got it.' That's all I needed, so that's airlift, rescue, CAS, that's the whole thing around the airfield. And the Rangers only moved out to secure the airfield, maybe a klick. So, we never got further than maybe a klick from Rio Hado. It's not like we put in an assault force and they were going to maneuver across the battlefield. The job was to secure and seize the airfield. I'm sure you did that kinda thing with the 82d when you were with the 14 ASOS?"

"Sure," I replied.

"In the complexity of an airfield," LA continued, "That's where it would have really required you to be in G with whatever combat control element you had there. In other words if you were with the 82d and you were maneuvering across the battlefield in Iraq, that's a traditional close air support, TACP/ALO kinda thing, and there's nobody better in the world. But when you put in an airfield, it just makes it more complex. And I'm sure you may or may not have deferred to the Combat Controllers," LA laughs.

"Yes sir, they were integral to every single thing the XVIIIth or 82d ever did. It was always the first question, 'Where are those guys?"

"Right. So, and that's a traditional combat control mission, on the airfield. A traditional combat control mission is not forward air control, it's on the airfield, it's really airfields, I mean it's our origin, it's our history. It's only in the Special Ops world, with Special Ops teams that you get that they now see that as their sole mission, but the real origin of combat control had everything to do with tactical airlift, like everything, that was the focus. We know that's not the focus now, but that's what it was. And we had great pararescuemen and combat controllers that provided emergency care to Rangers that were shot. It is the first time I'd seen a no kidding real sucking chest wound. And I realized that's why they call it a sucking chest wound, cause a Ranger wasn't sure what it was or how he was shot, or whatever, but he no kidding had a hole in his chest, I'd say no kidding about four inches in diameter and our pararescue guys were trying to save him and threw him on the hood of one of these little ATV type vehicles that we had. We didn't save him, but in all my years up to that point I'd never seen a sucking chest wound. Our pararescue guys couldn't save him.

We did provide BDA on the 117 drops to the 12th Air Force commander; he didn't like the BDA, because my BDA was 'Combat Effective.' So I get a report back that says, 'That's not BDA. BDA is tell me how the building was blown up, how many people we killed...' So, the way I understood it, our target was the barracks, so it hits maybe seventy five to a hundred meters to the south of the building and scared the shit out, apparently, the entire battalion and they un-assed the building and ran up into the woods. So, they could have stayed and fought, I don't know, maybe some of them did or some of them didn't, so I didn't know how to say it at the time, but that barracks was supposed to be filled, and when we got there it wasn't. So, that's how I reported the BDA – Combat Effective. That didn't go over well, because they wanted to know damage, and all that, but we didn't destroy the building. So, I don't know and when Feast tells the story, I tell him from the ground perspective. We actually had a young Captain, name of Jeff Shultize, stand in the crater and we took a picture, and at the time we didn't have digital cameras, so we took the picture and couldn't get it developed until we got back. We provided that to 12th Air Force. I don't where that ended up in the history books, but there was that picture of Jeff Shultize standing in the bottom of that crater for the F-117 drops, which is pretty cool.

We had a lot of problems; you know, at Rio Hado, a lot of issues that required Airmen and Airmen only to do. We were doing combat offloading from 130s and the commander of airlift forces – we didn't call them DIRMOBFORs back then, we called the COMALFs, commander of airlift forces, they basically worked for the CFACC and we didn't call them CFACCs back then. The 12th Air Force commander was the C-NAF, the Combat Numbered Air Force commander, and the COMALF, which was normally out of 21st Air Force, worked for the CFACC but again we didn't call them that back then, the 12th Air Force commander. So, they reported back to COMALF that everything had to be a combat offload. So, if you're an airlift guy, they don't like combat offloads, since you're never turning off your engines, you're basically taxiing into position and you're always going to be on a roll, and they push the pallets out. And the COMALF wanted to know why I was doing that. Well, because there's still a threat, it's not significant, there's personnel, you know one single mortar round, one single mortar round can ruin our whole day. You think about one single mortar round hitting that C-130, it would take out the whole airfield basically. So, COMALF was upset with me. The very next day during a combat offload, as soon as the 130 takes off, a mortar round, bam, right on the taxiway, right where the 130 would have been, twenty five seconds before. That would have been a big I told you so. If you're the primary air traffic controller, that's not what I wanted to be known for, the guy that got the C-130 on the airfield blown up. That's just not how I wanted to be remembered. Rangers used counter-mortar, and actually counter-mortar is one of the best things to use. My ALO again tried to bring in the A-37! I said, how do you mark the target, how do you know where it is? The reason counter mortar works is you're basically going mortar v. mortar, and you're WAG'ing is a little bit better than trying to direct an A-37 onto a target. It's jungle by the way. So, that's just one of those things that we had to work out. And I don't know if the counter-mortar was good, but we stopped getting shelled, so, I think it worked.

So, that's where I'm not always anti-Army, you know what the Army wants to do, sometimes it makes a lot of sense, especially if you're being shot at. I think you would have made the assessment after that mission that I would never have gone into the Air Force TACP, right? And then I found out, when the Combat Controllers were doing the history, they talked to him when he was at the Air Staff I think, he said, 'Don't ever tell LA that I was at Rio Hado.' I said, 'What? I don't remember him being there with me.' But, later he said, 'Yeah, I was the one that called in that A-37, I was with the ALO there.' I didn't find that out until, maybe a year and half ago, that he was there with me. I thought I knew every single guy, that I touched them, like every single Air Force guy, so, I never figured out where he was, but he was the guy that called in the A-37."

LA continued a great career as a Special Tactics Officer (STO) and Air Liaison Officer (ALO) and many other staff and command positions. He served in the Pentagon, the White House and commanded two Wings that were firsts in the USAF, the 484th AEW and the 93 AGOW. He retired as a Brigadier General.

DESERT STORM
17 January 1991 – 28 February 1991

Under dictator Saddam Hussein, the Iraqi Army invaded and occupied Kuwait on 2 August 1990. The US's relationship with Iraq had gone from negative to positive and back and forth over the years since the Cold War. During the Iran-Iraq war we backed Iraq, supplying some funds, supplies and limited armaments. Iraq claimed that Kuwait was rightfully one of its provinces and had been garnering oil revenues, which were rightfully Iraq's. Kuwait offered to pay nine of the ten billion demanded. Hussein ordered the attack. Iraqi units, led by commandos, crossed the border and after two days of intense fighting, began occupying the country. Operation Desert Shield began on 7 August 1990 and the US began mobilizing a large multi-service force to the region. Eventually, the United Nations Security Council passed Resolution 678 on 29 November 1990, directing the use of all means necessary to remove Iraqi forces from Kuwait. The Resolution gave the Iraqis until 15 January 1991 to withdraw. The United States formed the backbone of a multi-national coalition consisting of 34 countries. On 17 January 1991 Operation Desert Storm kicked off with an air campaign that lasted 44 days, flying 100,000 sorties at the cost of 75 coalition aircraft. On 24 February 1991 150,000 coalition troops and 1500 tanks crossed the borders of Kuwait and Iraq. On 27 February, Saddam ordered the retreat from Kuwait. As they retreated Saddam ordered the torching of over 700 oil wells.

When it was over, approximately 500 coalition personnel were killed and between 20,000-30,000 Iraq military were killed. About 5000 Kuwaiti and Iraqi civilians were also killed during the short conflict. The aftermath of the Gulf War lingers on as veterans suffer from Gulf War syndrome and although opinions remain mixed, the effects of depleted uranium. In what turned out to be the showcase for "smart weapons," approximately 25% of the coalition casualties were caused by friendly fire.

Vet: *"Shack"*
Setting: *Shack's Up-State New York home outside of Watertown, New York, home of the US Army's 10th Mountain Division, some of the best white water rafting in the country and a bunch of defunct paper mills. Shack's house was unique, supposedly owned at one point by Al Capone's brother, or cousin or accountant, something like that. The house was on eleven acres and had a full-up, no shit, top notch waterfall running through in the backyard. Shack loved the place and whenever we got together there we sat outside, no matter what time of year, made a fire, drank and bullshitted. This time it was at night, in December. The waterfall was about fifty percent frozen, the fire was blazing and there wasn't a cloud in the sky.*
Drinks: *Shack – Glenmorangie, "The Original," a ten-year-old single malt, scent and taste are fruity, me – the same. We both also simultaneously drank Millers and smoked run of the mill cigars with our fine Scotch.*

Story: There he was... Shack and I chit chatted for a while and one thing led to another and he asked me if he'd ever told me his Desert Storm story, which he'd told me three or four times before, but I never got tired of hearing it or drinking and smoking with my friend, so I said, "No."

"Yeah, it was right before Desert Storm and I was an ALO at Shaw with the 21st TAS, aligned with the 82d. So, in August of 1990, Saddam invades Kuwait. I'm at the end of my three-year assignment there at Shaw and I had an assignment to go to Luke. So my squadron commander calls me and a goes, 'Hey Shack, they just mobilized the 82d, but you've got this class date in September, so I'll tell you what I'm gonna do. I'm gonna yank you out of the 82d and align you with an Armor unit from Europe, 'cause there's no way those guys are going. You go off and get checked out in the F-16, maybe you can catch this war from the pointy end.

I high-fived him and said, boss that sounds like a great idea. So that was that, they realigned me to a different unit, the 1st Armored Division. No shit, less than a week later he calls me back in and tells me they just mobilized the 1st Armored Division, and says, 'You gotta go.'

Ok boss. And I gotta leave in about three weeks. So, I had to go hook up with our unit in Germany, who I'd never met before, didn't know any of these guys. It was right after Thanksgiving, we ship out to Germany, spend a few weeks waiting for our movement orders to get into Saudi Arabia. It was a few days before

Christmas and we deploy with our Army unit, end up at Al Dhafra, Saudi Arabia.

Khobar Towers was where we were billeted. The plumbing there was Middle East plumbing, one inch pipes, versus the three inch pipes that the US uses, because in that part of the world they don't use toilet paper. They had this bidet type thing and a toilet. Everything in there was gold plated. Everything there was vacant. The Saudis had built these things for the Bedouins, because they were trying to get them to move out of the desert so they could have more control over them, but they refused to live in these buildings. So, we get into these buildings and pretty soon a couple thousand soldiers start flushing the toilets with toilet paper, and it plugs up all the pipes and all the floors start flooding, the shit is running down the walls. After a few days of this our Battalion commander says, "This is bullshit, we're getting out of here too." So we ended up driving 20 miles out into the desert and setting up camp. This is where we started working out how the formations would move, all the shoot, move and communicate stuff. It was a lot of fun, it was Army living, MREs everyday, a couple of liters of water, but I thought it was cool.

It was during this time I got to know the Battalion Commander, LTC John Wedawhich and he let me know what his philosophy was. He told me 'You bring more firepower than all of the tanks in one of my Battalions, so I need you to stay alive.' So he says, 'So here's the plan, once we get into the battle, and we will get into a battle, I want you to follow me. If we're going through mine fields, put one track in one of my tracks, that way we'll reduce the chances of you hitting a mine by fifty percent. If we start taking fire, get on the downwind side of that fire and he said his vehicle would shield mine. He also said, if your vehicle does get hit and you're still alive, I want you to grab your portable radios, jump into my vehicle, I'll kick out my gunner and you'll ride with me, because I need you.' So I said, ok, sure sir, but I don't know how to shoot a 50 Cal. He said, 'We'll take care of that.' So we go out in the desert and they taught me how to load an M1A1 for this emergency situation. It took about two rounds, and I got it, take it load it, boom, boom."

Shack downs his Scotch, picks up his beer, takes a swig and puts it back down next to his chair. He reaches down on the other side and picks up the Scotch bottle, pulls the cork and leans over to pour me more and then refills his. He continues...

"So, we were 2nd Brigade of 1/35 Armor. There was going to be a unit ahead of us, of Battalion sized strength in our corridor and they were going to clean up any sporadic stuff, but we, the center of mass, was going after the Medina Division, Republican Guard. We knew where they were, they'd been pinned down, they'd been bombed for several weeks, so we knew pretty much where they were and that was our target. As we got within, maybe 20 klicks of their position we do a passage of lines, in Army speak, and then we were going to be the go-get-em guys. So, uh, the day comes we were going to cross the berm, all the units are lined up, they had the engineering units blow lanes across the minefields and then we'd go single file as we penetrated the minefields. One we'd get to the other side at a safe distance, we'd spread out again into attack formation. So, there's a thousand stories about all that kinda stuff. The day comes and I'm trying to think of something. This is just so cool, I gotta do something. The theme song from Patton comes to mind, you know, da da da daa da da da dump da daa, wouldn't that be so cool as soon as we're crossing from Saudi into Iraqi I key the mic and play that song. Well I happened to have a whole box of cassette tapes, and on one of those tapes I had military songs and one of those songs was that song. So, I went to Col Wedawhich and I said, *Hey boss, would you mind, this is a motivational thing, how about as we cross the berm I key the mic...* He says, 'That's a great idea Air Force, why didn't I think of that?'

"So, it was our turn, I'm following the commander's tank and he's the first one in our Battalion to go across, and I'm following right in close trail behind 'em and just as we're going over the top of the first berm, his call sign was Tiger 6, so I go, "Tiger 6 this is ALO," whatever our call sign was, "Ready." He goes, "Go for it Air Force!" So, I key the mic and do the, da da da daa da da da dump da daa... and we clear through, get to the other side and a bunch of Army guys came up to me and said, "Man that was sweat!" So, it was all about knowing your job and you gotta get along with the guys you're with and that was one of the small steps of showing them, hey we're in this together. So, another thing I thought would be cool, because we had this GPS, since we could tell where we were real time, I would mark our positions every thirty minutes as we went across this featureless desert and if we came up alongside something significant, like a blown up truck or whatever, I could mark that position and I had an acetate map so I was marking it all with a grease pencil, or I think a Sharpie. I'll show you that map sometime if I can find it in the attic."

Shack downs his Scotch, picks up his beer, takes a swig and puts it back down next to his chair. He again reaches down on the other side and picks up the Scotch bottle, pulls the cork and leans over to pour me more and then refills his. He continues...

"For example, if we came up on an enemy position, these guys were living out in the desert for weeks, getting bombed and they were in no mood to fight, so we had a lot of POWs that we were trying to corral, I'd write a note like, sixty POWs, for whoever was doing the recovery for these guys. Or we came upon a BMP that was on a suicidal mission that came across our formation hit by M1A1, four KIA, so I have these notations as we're marching along. So, everything is going as planned, actually there was a logistics plan, it was supposed to take us four or five days to get up to and get into position to hit the Medina Division. That was with the assumption we were going to hit a lot of resistance. Well, there wasn't any. We just rolled through. So, the decision was made to just roll for 24/7 until we got into position. So, as we were doing this we ran into a fuel problem. I mean right out of the Battle of the Bulge scenario, here we are with the Battalion commander bitching about, 'Hey man we got to get those tankers up here because I'm going to run out of gas...' We gotta go, we know where they are, we're going to surprise them, but now we've got no gas. The HEMETs, these big tankers, they're refueling a whole bunch of people in the same position, so it was a fuel problem. So we went as far as we could, what turned out to be the night before the battle, we had to stop because we didn't have the gas. There's this raging storm going on, we're on the higher desert so there's this rain, snow mix, fifty knot winds blowing mud; really bizarre conditions and nobody's slept in a couple of days. You're trying to get some rest, sleeping for a few minutes here and there, resting your helmet on the radio and falling asleep for a few seconds, we were all just a bunch of stunned mullets at this point, passengers in some sardine can waiting for some battle that's about to happen. But, you don't know, what's a battle going to be like? I'd never been in a battle before.

So, we end up getting fuel and it's a couple hours before daylight when we get the order that we're pressing on. Most of the guys are still napping. We're moving at maybe 10 knots, 12 miles per hour was about as fast as we could go. And the vehicle I was in was an M113 track and everyone else in the formation were either in M1A1s or in Bradleys, which certainly had more protection than the 113. We just had an aluminum skin, basically it would protect you against small arms fire, and that's about it. So, this is where the plan comes into effect, if we start taking any real fire protect ourselves as much as we can by shielding ourselves behind the armored vehicles. What I didn't know sitting in my track, was how close the Medina Division was. In my mind it was still seven, eight, nine miles away, but in fact they were a lot closer. So, I was personally surprised when all of a sudden the chatter starts getting up to critical mass on the radios and I could tell that some of our units were getting a lot of hotspots on their thermal sights in the tanks. So there was something right in front of us. And at this point, it hadn't quite registered in my mind that it was game on. The plan was to get on line, this was a sloping desert, where the terrain would vary by about fifty, sixty feet up and down with some areas of good visibility and other areas that were pockets. Because I had the GPS I would radio Tiger 6 and relay our position and he used that as a tool to keep everybody else on line. Because, you couldn't see the guys on your far right, and you couldn't see the guys on your far left, but the idea was to keep us in a straight line to hit the Medina Division. So, as we start rolling forward, we start taking our first artillery fire. I'd been briefed by some crusty old Soldier, "If you see something different out here on the desert and explosions are happening, like around an old junk car or a clump of trees... don't be anywhere near those because they probably already gridded out all of the approaches to their position and they use those little terrain features as their zeroing spots. So, they'll lob shells, see where they hit and make adjustments with their forward observers to where you are." I listened to what he said, but it didn't register what that really meant. So, as we roll forward, and I'm doing my Air Force stuff, you know, what airplanes are available, what's the weather like, but at this point there's no way I figure I'd need to call in airstrikes. But I still had all my stuff laid out."

Shack pauses to put in a dip. Readjusts the chew until it's comfortable, then spits.

"So, we stop. I don't know why, I'm just an Air Force dude in this track. As we're sitting there in this formation, all of a sudden, whaa booomm! And the track shakes a little bit, and you here this, jee jee jee, and my ROMAD who's up on the 50 CAL, drops his head down into the track and he's covered with dirt. His name was Fundy, so I said, "Fundy, what happened?" He goes, "Uhhh, big explosion." So, I pop my head out of the track and literally twenty to thirty meters in front of us there's a whole in front of us the size of a half a swimming pool. So, it took awhile, you know, slow Air Force guy, to figure out it was some kind of artillery shell. Then within a few seconds, kaa boom!, another one behind us, about twice the distance as the first one away and more dirt raining down on top of us. It's like what the hell, trying to sort out what's going on here and then I notice there are Bradleys, and we were using Bradleys as our perimeter defense, and their job was to go after any dismounts, or light skinned vehicles using their lighter weaponry and the tanks are going to go after the armor. So, I notice these Bradleys are backing up. As I'm looking at the Bradleys I see this orange painted garbage can sitting in the desert maybe fifty to hundred meters from our position and then the flash came back what that soldier told me, if you see something like that they're probably zeroing in. I yelled to our driver, who was an Army guy, "Back up, back up, back up!" So, he slams it into reverse, not like at seventy miles an hour, we're backing up at like ten miles an hour. A half a dozen more rounds came in, not effective fire, but, you're watching this happen, explosions going off around you, you're like, I guess this is what a battle is like, but, no that's not what a battle was like, that was just the beginning.

So, we reset the lines. There was some counter-fire that was called in and this was all learning on the fly, what ground tactics were. I mean guys were firing counter-fire to suppress the artillery fire. Within a short period of time we started rolling forward again. As we roll forward, the Battalion commander looks at me and says, 'Ok Air Force, remember what I told you.' So, we get into this attack formation and we start rolling over this crest, this sand dune. The visibility was probably a klick or less and all of a sudden you hear a couple of calls over the radio, 'I've got a contact, 090 at six hundred meters.' The Battalion commander says, 'Confirm. Fire.' Within a minute you hear all these other tanks calling in targets and the Battalion commander essentially says, ok, those are all bad guys out there, fire for effect, if you see anything shoot it. Since we're all on the line, anything in front of us are bad guys, all the good guys are behind us. So, now there's a lot of firing going on, you can see off in the distance these fireballs going up, kinda fuzzy, but you can make it out. So, the tactic that he was using, we knew we could out range the T-72s, but we had to figure out where that range was, so we would roll forward very slowly, shooting. Occasionally we'd see something kick up in the dirt around us. The soldiers knew what that was. Those were rounds coming in from the T-72s, so we'd stop and start backing up maybe one hundred meters and start engaging. Once that enemy fire stopped we'd roll forward another hundred meters. That's how we proceeded as we approached the Medina Division. Everything started to come into view, burning T-72. And off to our right was this huge mound, which turned out to be an ammo dump. As this battle is going on there are explosions coming out of this ammo dump and periodically I'm sticking my head up out of the track and talking on the radio, trying to figure out what air is available. As I'm sticking my head out at one point I look over at this ammo dump, I see a big fireball coming up out of the ammo dump. I see something flying through the air and it's surreal, this thing is tumbling as it closer and closer to you and then a piece hits the ground – I look at it and it's the size of a refrigerator, and it had just come from about a kilometer away! Now I'm cinching up my helmet, figuring I'm going to get hit in the head with something here.

As we're moving forward the Bradleys on our right side started vectoring thirty degrees to the left to go around this exploding ammo dump and at the same time we're taking fire from this ditch which is near the perimeter of the ammo dump. So, we'd see guys pop up out of the ditch and you'd see a corkscrew smoke trail, which is what you'd figure an RPG looks like, when it's coming right at you. But, it was totally ineffective, falling hundreds of meters short, it sounded like an M-80 going off, but, you knew those guys were shooting at you. Now air starts checking in. I ask the Battalion commander if he's got any targets for me. He says, "You know Air Force, I think we've got everything we can see, but I can't target what I can't see. So, you got a plan for that?" So, I suggested we bring the air in, have them fly over us to identify who we are to them, then I'll release the fighters, under flight lead control, to go beyond our trace and go kill stuff on the other side. In order for them to identify us, I need to give them a visual. So, I said, "Hey sir, when they fly over our front line trace we need to mark our position with smoke." With a tank they release oil into their turbine and it generates a whole bunch of smoke, for this exact purpose – somebody thought this through. So, on my mark, I'm talking to the fighters, first set were A-10s, I tell them on my mark plus thirty seconds we'll release smoke. The vis was really shitty, a 4000 foot overcast and the A-10s were flying below the ceiling, but as soon as everybody hit their smoke, flight lead calls in a says he's got us visual. So, I tell them, those are the good guys. If you go forward of our position 500 meters, you'll see a bunch of burning hulks. Pilot comes back and tells me he's got it and they're going to start hitting those targets and anything beyond. So, they start making multiple passes, coming in right over our heads. At that point, they shot their mavericks. You'd see that big ass missile come off the rails and a few seconds later, maybe two klicks beyond us you'd hear and see secondaries. The pilots confirmed after that first pass that they had plenty of targets. Another four-ship comes in and I get them to start shooting and now everybody is doing their job. After a couple of cycles of this, they ran out of targets. There were SAMs in the area, so we didn't want them to go too deep. They stayed in the vicinity of our front lines, plus maybe a kilometer.

Now I'm out of the track, cause I've got to keep the fighters in sight. There are two Bradleys on either side of us. As I'm looking out I see the Bradley on the right of us. A small puff of smoke pops up on the front of the Bradley. I said to myself, huh, I wonder what that was. Within a few seconds, I can see a little smoke coming out of the Bradley, doesn't look like much, just a little smoke, but then more smoke. All of sudden the back hatch drops open and a dude falls out the back and starts belly crawling away from the vehicle across the desert. I thought, huh, must have gotten hit. He stops, gets up, runs back into the Bradley and grabs what I thought was a duffle bag out of the back of the track and starts dragging it across the desert. Turns out the duffle bag was actually a guy missing his legs. Wow, I guess fights on. So, I continue to work the fighters as we roll forward. I couple of minutes later I look and the same thing happens to the Bradley on the left. I just happened to be looking that way and see that same puff of smoke at the front of the vehicle. This time, three guys immediately jump out and start running. Now we're taking hits.

So, I'm thinking, here I am, I'm a fighter pilot, my dad was in the Army, he was in a tank Battalion that ended up on the Pusan perimeter in Korea, and I'm thinking he probably thought, being a typical Army guy, "You guys don't know what it's like, flying your airplanes, you don't know what it's like to be down here in a tank battle." And here I am in a tank battle, trying to figure out how I got here and what are my odds of making it out – cause we just started and we've got a long way to go. So, all these thought are running through my mind. But, I still had a job to do and I figured the best way to get out of this alive was to just keep going forward and do your job and kill them before they kill you. But, I will say though, that anytime something very intense was happening, it was amazing the clarity that comes in for brief periods of time. All of a sudden everything is in slow motion, it's crystal clear, everything makes perfect sense and you just do it. It's when things slow down that you have to worry, because now these other thoughts come back into your cranium. Then something else will happen and you get that clarity back, then slows down, thoughts come back, back and forth, back and forth. And this isn't happening over a period of hours; it's over maybe twenty or thirty minutes. So, you have these snapshots burned into your brain – this happened, then this happened, just weird biology going on there.

So, now we're at the point we ran out of targets for the aircraft and the weather is getting shittier. I recommended we knock off any more air until we get more targets and the weather cleared a bit. The Battalion commander was good with that. One of the four-ships of A-10s that checked in with us, we heard over the radio that one of them was having some hydraulic problem and everything seemed calm and normal so they were going to back out of the IP and go sort it out. We heard he had hydraulic failure, manual reversion. They checked out with us and last we heard he was going back to base. At about the same time a four-ship of F-16s checks in. I told them to hold west of the IP since we didn't have any valid targets at that time, so stand by. Then there was a flurry of activity from a Battalion to the left of us. The flight lead decided he was going to go in to help them, he was now talking to another controller in that Battalion and flew right over us on their way to them. Within thirty seconds of them flying over us, we hear an emergency beacon going off, chatter on the emergency frequency, 'Lead is going down, no chute, no chute...' Then we heard bits and pieces over the radio chatter, '...I'm in the chute, I'm good, I'm at 500 feet...hey, they're shooting at me...' It all goes quiet. Then we hear from one of the flight members, it was number three I think, he took over the flight lead duties and we hear him talking to the guy on the ground, but we can't here the guy on the ground talking to him, other than mic breaks. So, number three is keeping the flight circling overhead. As this is going on, we're communicating with HQ and ask for a helicopter to go get him. We really don't know what's going on, but we know they're now sending in a helicopter to get this downed Airmen. This is all focused chaos at this point. We hear a call over the radio, '...break right, break right!' Then the F-16 flight lead says, "We're bingo gas, gotta go, rescue forces on the way." So, we continued on with our day. All we knew was we had a guy on the ground, the flight capped until they ran out of gas and we possibly had a rescue chopper going to pick him up.

We continue to march forward and we start coming up on all the wreckage, it was carnage, burning vehicles, body parts – big chunks, little chunks – went right passed a guy who'd gotten run over by a tank. It was cartoonish; all the fluids had been squished out of his body. He was like a road kill that had been on the road for a while, but the part of his body that hadn't gotten run over was all bloated and his hand was sticking out of the dirt. It was just carnage everywhere. We roll forward, minimal resistance. Now we get passed the main area of the battle, so now we're on the far side of it. This is where we get the order to stop. So we just stop. Now it's getting dark out. We had a huddle with the command staff. They said, "Ok, we've been told to stay here until further orders." It's amazing how you can sleep with all this going on. You can fall asleep in thirty seconds and sleep for five minutes and swear it was eight hours, and get up and you're good to go again. Just about everybody out there was in the same position as me, they hadn't been in battles either, except for maybe some old crusty Sergeant Majors from Vietnam. They worked through the night to get us food and gas, cause they think we're going to press forward to the Euphrates River the next day. So, we're all just sitting there. It's midnight and we get the word that the ground war is going to end at 0700 the following morning. We were in disbelief; we thought we had days left of this. Nope, war's over at 0700 in the morning. We got the word from the S3, the MLRS Battalion behind us has got thousands of rounds and they've been told, "...don't bring them back." So, they're going to fire them all off at 0600 in the morning. They'd gridded out depots around us and any concentrations of troops that hadn't given up yet. They were just going to launch everything – and they've got cluster munitions, these were the big guns. But, they set up less than a klick behind us. This was going to be a hell of a show. So everybody got out on their vehicles or cots, laying on the desert looking up at the sky. They launch thousands of these rockets. It just reminded me of a scene out of the old show The World At War, when the Russians were hitting the Germans and there were these massive barrages, constant flashes and booms, flashes and booms, completely surreal. There were so many shots going off it was like a setting sun hitting a thunderstorm. You'd see off on the horizon, hundreds and thousands of flashes on the horizon as these things hit their targets. Fweeshh, fweeshh, fweeshh; frickin incredible. Sure enough, at 0700 all shooting ceases. It was like turning off the TV, everything stopped. So we gathered up stuff. Then I heard what happened with the F-16 pilot. They couldn't find him. Two helicopters were shot down trying to go get him. The A-10 that we thought was good to go, went back to base and tried to land in manual reversion. The manual will tell you don't try to land an A-10 in manual reversion, but several weeks prior somebody had done it, who had a similar problem and survived. This guy went back and when he was coming in for a landing, he didn't have enough flight control, the aircraft tumbled and he was killed. So, the guy we thought that was certainly dead, we didn't know what his status was, and the guy we thought was ok was dead. Fast forward to a couple of weeks later. Turns out the guy that got shot down was a good friend of mine, Bill Andrews. He had been captured and tortured. Funny story about his wife, by the way, Bill just died this year of cancer, his wife was a real firecracker. She's at her home in Germany when the staff car pulls up with the Chaplain and the Wing commander she opens up the curtain, sees them, knows exactly what this means, so she opens the door. The Wing commander is giving his pitch, she says, "Say whatever the fuck you've got to say to me, then get the fuck out of my house." Bill survived the war, but the first that Stacey knew he was alive was when CNN had a shot of him coming down the staircase of an aircraft after he was released. After everything calmed down, we spent the better part of the next few days just driving around to all the burnt out hulks, bodies, body parts and just calling out a mark and filling out a log with these ten-digit grids that we're passing on and hand that over to the body recovery teams. Sometimes the body recovery team would show up, find a dead Iraqi's wallet, pull out id cards, you know it was sad, they were the bad guys, but now the war was over, so you got to see all that.

Morale of the story, most incredible event of my life and wouldn't trade it for anything."

That was just the near beginning of Shack's nearly 30 year career. He flew OV-10s, F-111s and F-16s, commanded a Squadron and a Group and was in key operational positions for both Operation Enduring Freedom in Afghanistan and Operation Iraqi Freedom. He finished up his career in an important staff job and transitioned after retirement into Government Service.

Operation Enduring Freedom
7 October 2001 – December 2014

Operation Enduring Freedom was primarily the US response to the attacks of 11 September 2001. The goal was to destroy terrorist training facilities, capture Al Qaeda leadership and prevent further terrorist activity in Afghanistan. The air portion of OEF began on 7 October 2001 and consisted of strikes against terrorist facilities and Taliban fielded forces. Special Operations forces were on the ground to assist the local tribal leaders in fighting the Taliban and regaining control of their country. There were several phases of OEF, the first culminated in the capture of Kabul and Kandahar in late 2001. Several attempts were made to rout Taliban leadership and kill or capture Osama Bin Laden. A showdown occurred in early 2002 with the first large scale conventional forces to operate in Afghanistan and the remnants of Al Qaeda formed foreign fighters in what became know as Operation Anaconda. In the twelve years since, the success of military and nation building efforts has been hard to gauge. OEF-Afghanistan official came to an end in December of 2014. Coalition forces still fight there today under a different operation, but they are there nonetheless. In all almost two-dozen countries fought in the international coalition against Al Qaeda and Taliban forces at a cost of over 13,000 killed and approximately 25,000 enemy forces.

The Afghanistan experience is unique. Afghanistan has the historical reputation of being a destroyer of armies, back to the time of Alexander. On one of my tours there I was bartering with a local to purchase an old rifle. Being interested in history and old weapons this one caught my eye. It turned out it was a British rifle from the retreat from Kabul in January of 1842. Of the over 16,000 British and Indian personnel (12,000 were families and camp followers) only one British soldier survived. The Soviet Army fell in Afghanistan. When I got on the ground in Afghanistan in early December of 2001 I was taken by the history of the country and also fell in love with the people and the landscape. At that time, shortly after 9/11 we still felt, or I'll say, I felt like a liberator. We were out amongst the people and made a connection. It was romantic. After a couple tours, we armored up, built FOBs (Forward Operating Bases) and most of us anyway, distanced ourselves from the people. There were still our Special Operators trying to maintain that connection. The troops that got involved in training the Afghans maintained that connection, but the average trooper, Airman, Marine or Sailor was focused on holding ground, securing, killing and capturing.

I actually think we won in Afghanistan. I think we won in late 2002 or early 2003. I remember reading an article in the paper that highlighted that Al Qaeda was giving up efforts in Afghanistan because of our successes and the Afghan resistance. Then we shifted our focus to Iraq.

Vet: *Jason*

Setting: *This conversation occurred over the phone.*

Drinks: *Jason wasn't drinking; I had a turmeric and ginger green tea (it's for medicinal purposes).*

Story: "This actually starts back in 1994. I'll show you how it all comes around. I don't know, I think it's my own personal Moby Dick story I've been pondering over the years.

I was commissioned in 1993 and went through the Infantry Officer's Basic Course and everything. My first assignment was the Republic of Panama. I was 5/87th Infantry, Fort Davis. Panama was very much an old school assignment. We were a separate infantry battalion; we had been a separate infantry brigade, but they shut down the other battalion. We were this lone battalion, sort of on the bad side of Panama. It was just a depressed area, high crime rate, what have you. It was almost like you were in the 1950's Army over there. The soldiers would hang out in brothels on the weekend, because that was all that was around the base, were these brothels. You were allowed to be in the bars downstairs, but you weren't allowed to go upstairs, you know, where they actually did business. The MPs would walk through all the brothels to ensure all of the soldiers remained downstairs, but really, the MPs were using the brothels along with everybody else. I mean everybody just wanted the soldiers to stay in their rooms with the girls when they were walking through.

It was just; it was really a bizarre place. All the things that were going on in the rest of the world seemed to be leaving Panama behind. It was a fairly depressed country while being relatively Americanized. Thanks to the end of the Cold War, we had an Army without a purpose. Our job in Panama was to protect the Panama Canal, but who from? It was the end of the Cold War, it was before the War on Terror, you really had a military without a purpose and our battalion was sort of a microcosm of what was going on, I think, to the rest of the military.

In the middle of all that, you had Haiti collapsing into chaos. You basically had the government collapse and Haitian refugees were fleeing on boats to the US. The US policy was to always to turn around the Haitians and send them home. We just hadn't seen Haitians in numbers like these fleeing the country. So, it created a big issue for the government. There were simply too many to keep rounding them up and sending them back. We're trying to sort out what to do with all these refugees and in the middle of all of that Fidel Castro who's really clever about global politics and always knew how to make the US look bad, started encouraging his malcontents to take to the ocean, because he knew that the US policy toward Haitians was very different than the US policy toward Cuban refugees. Castro started sending folks out on boats and the US found itself in a hypocritical position, you know, refugees are refugees and if anything the Haitian refugees were leaving a lot worse case than the Cuban refugees. They didn't know what to do with them. The US solution was to get Haiti back on its feet, so we planned the invasion of Haiti and in the meantime all the refugees, Haitian and Cuban, we would put in refugee camps. So, Guantanamo Bay was quickly over filling with refugees and they needed some place to send some of the refugees.

They sent several thousand Cuban refugees to Panama on a voluntary basis to be housed in refugee camps there. So the Cuban refugees were sent to the camps, they weren't happy about coming. I don't know what they were told, how that might help their chances of getting accepted into the US, but my battalion, which otherwise didn't have much to do in the world, was given the mission of preparing to assist with security in the camps. And there were going to be four camps. As I recall there was an Army camp, and Air Force camp, a Navy camp and I can't remember what the fourth one was; it might have been that there were two Army camps. Our battalion would be basically providing perimeter security. The camps were built on Empire Range, which was the range complex where do all of our shooting. It was across the Panama Canal across from Panama City. It was relatively isolated. You had a road alongside the canal, otherwise you had pretty thick rainforest, people will call it jungle, but it was actually rainforest. It was a good way to isolate the refugees and basically, control them.

Marines came over from Gitmo where they'd been basically handling refugees too, to advise and assist all of us as the camps were being built. They were really just concrete pallets with GP larges (tents) just thrown up for the refugees with the typical camp layouts in the four camps, with just chain link fences surrounding them. The Marines took one look at it and were somewhere between horrified and somewhat mystified that we had no notion how to house refugees. They explained that we needed triple strength concertina wire, that we needed to do all these things for our own security, at a fairly senior level, but I was only a second lieutenant so I didn't know who was saying what to who, but at a fairly senior level the decision was made that we weren't running prison camps, that we treat the refugees as guests. The Marines, sort of left in defeat, saying, 'Good luck.'

We prepared for the refugees. I had been a reservist in high school. I had joined the Army reserves between my junior and senior years of high school and I joined the 442nd Infantry in Hawaii and had a lot of state pride, since it was the all-Japanese unit during World War II and at the time they were actually located across from the Hale Koa, right there at Fort Derussy. I had gotten civil disturbance operations training in my reserve unit. It turned, that in my company, there were only a couple of us that had ever done actual civil disturbance training before, who understood just the basics of it. Believe it or not, the manual on CD operations is actually good manual. You could actually just open it up and learn quite a bit. You still needed a good hands-on understanding of it. We did what we could to train, but it really, there really just wasn't the experience to properly prepare for the kind of civil disturbance ops situations that the Marines warned us that would be coming. As a second lieutenant I'd tell the company commander my concerns, but to him I was just some dumb second lieutenant fresh out of West Point, so what did I know. I was just some officer's officer that was to him being cocky for explaining what we were doing was inadequate. I did what I could to train my platoon. I was in a really good position because normally you show up as a second lieutenant and you're playing catch up the whole time. As a second lieutenant you'll know the latest in terms of doctrine and maybe some of the newest techniques being fielded to the Army, because you just got out of school. But beyond that the expectation is, that you're a second lieutenant so do your best not to make too many waves. You learn what you can. Everybody tries to wrap second lieutenants in bubble wrap as much as they can. And as a second lieutenant it's your job to fight through that and actually be a leader. But there's always that back and forth tension. As a second lieutenant your job is not to sit in the corner but meanwhile your NCOs, just by the culture of the infantry especially, is to keep the lieutenant out of trouble. But in this case I was one of only two people in my platoon who had actually done civil disturbance stuff before, a lot of training I mean. It kinda gave me a cool in with my platoon where I could talk and they would actually listen.

I had an amazing platoon sergeant whose nickname was 'Triple Six,' you know as in the Anti-Christ. I mean he could be a pretty scary guy, he wasn't terribly tall in station or anything but he was a guy whose bark and bite were equally vicious. But, he and I quickly bonded; we were going to have these riots we were going to have to deal with. The company seems ill prepared for it we'll do what we can to get the platoon prepared for it but I mean civil disturbance operations are about mass. Twenty five guys can't really do anything you're supposed to be in a big mass of about a hundred and that in and of itself was one of the problems. We would train and move as a company, but more often it was go train as platoon which automatically told us we were screwed. We did what we could to get the company commander to listen, but we were going to train the platoon the best we can. We finally got some of the equipment we needed, but it really just came down to body shields and face shields. They weren't going to let us take shotguns with birdshot, which we normally would; we weren't going to bring in tear gas as you normally would. All the things that you would normally have to defeat a mob were the things they weren't going to let us have. At one point I was so frustrated that I was ready to go to the battalion commander, you know, literally throw my bars on the table and say we were walking into a disaster, blah, blah, blah. One of my squad leaders talked me out of it, '...nobody's gonna listen...' and he said the platoon is better off with me than without me, just let it go, we'll do our best. He basically talked me off the ledge.

On Dec 7, 1994 there was a big riot at one of the camps. We basically were alerted, we were on the opposite side of the canal, so we basically had to get our ruck sacks, get all of our equipment together, run out, wait for CH-47s to fly us out to the camp where basically demonstrators inside the camp had taken over the interior of the camp, guard blocks and everything, chasing them out. Our job was basically to go in and retake the camp. We went out to the pick up zone, we got on these 47s and flew down the Panama Canal to Empire range. It was really bizarre to see the company almost looking more like Roman Legionnaires, with the face shields, the body shields and the batons. Then we get on the helicopter to fly, it was this sort of anachronistic moment of combat, but not combat. I remember sitting in the CH-47 as we're flying down the canal, and they were flying low, all you could see on either side of the helicopter was the rainforest. You look down the row and all you see are soldiers all in their riot gear, it was just really odd.

So we landed and made our way out to the camp and basically surrounded the camp with our soldiers. With us as a sort of threat to the demonstrators, the camp commander then negotiated with them, trying to convince them to go back to the tents and trying to convince them to go back to waiting. That night we just sort of surrounded the camp and we heard that the refugees were mad because they had heard a rumor that some of the refugees were being allowed to travel to the US, and for some reason they weren't being allowed to travel to the US. Basically out of anger and frustration they had taken over the camp. I don't know the logic behind it, by violently demonstrating I don't actually know how they thought that would help them come to the country, but that was the situation. We were all kinda disappointed that we'd gotten all dressed up and told to stay outside the perimeter. At the same time my platoon sergeant and I reminded one another that going in would have been a disaster so it was just as well that we were being used as a threat.

The next morning talks broke down and the camp commander decided to commit us. We again asked about shotguns, we asked about tear gas and stuff and were told no. The order was my company would enter through one gate of the camp; it was more like a big platoon. An Air Force element of a comparable size would enter through a parallel gate. There's a big soccer field on one end of the camp where all of the demonstrators had mobbed. So, they wanted us to enter through these two gages. My company would go in and enter from one end of the soccer field going straight toward the other, so we would be in a line of platoon meeting with the Air Force element who would march straight out. So, we'd have the three riot platoons and the headquarters platoon meeting up with, like a massive platoon of the Air Force. That would force all the demonstrators back into the living are where all the tents were massed and would break up the mob, cause they wouldn't be able to group up with all the tents around, that was the theory. One of the problems was, to prevent erosion; all of the camps were covered in fist-sized rocks that came from a quarry nearby. So, the camps had an endless supply of missiles to hurl at us. And that's what the rioters had been using. Me and my platoon sergeant, when we'd gotten the word that we were going in and everything, basically we looked at one another and we knew we were fucked. After the excitement of flying out the day before, the realities of how precarious our situation was kinda returned and it was, yeah, this is gonna be bad. We didn't let the soldiers know that. We weren't going to do anything to demoralize them. We knew this was going to get really ugly.

We lined up and basically the order was 3rd platoon, 1st platoon, 2nd platoon and then headquarters. 3rd platoon would breach the gate, then my platoon would lead company in. We couldn't see the Air Force from where we were because there was a big dining facility between us. So, you had almost like two alleys leading into the soccer field. So, we lined up and we waited and we waited and we waited. We were there so long the demonstrators saw us and barricaded the gates and everything. Not that it would have been a big surprise, but any element of surprise was lost. Then they backed us off the gates for a while, then they sent us back up to the gates again, and then they committed us. When we marched in, 3rd platoon did its job of breaching the gate very quickly. The gate was opened and they pulled it open. As we were getting ready to go in, one of the first rocks hurled at us managed to hit me in the shin. We were in a column of threes, I had my three squad leaders in front of me, I was behind the center squad leader. It was kinda funny, looking back at it I was kinda glad I was the first one hit instead of one of the last ones, seemed better as a leader, but this rock comes in and hits me in the shin and I mean it almost knocks me down. I was like holy fuck. One of my guys looks at me, he's like, 'Sir, that looked like it hurt.' I was like, 'I'm fine,' and we started the march.

The gate actually opened to the backside of the dining facility. We kinda had to snake around, so we couldn't see the soccer field, we had to turn around the corner of the dining facility. So, first rock hits me, then a group of about a dozen people that were in front of the gate ran. Then we basically started marching. I was thinking, this isn't bad so far. Then we turn the corner and can actually see into the soccer field and there were hundreds of people in the soccer field. I'd seen in movies where they have archers shoot thousands of arrows down and you see this dark cloud of arrows coming down, it always makes me think about when we turned the corner because I saw the hundreds of people, and then the sky just filled with rocks. I mean it was just an insane sight to see all of that coming down on us. The rocks started just pouring down and smashing us. The platoon was very well trained. The platoon was trained to stay together and keep moving forward. We had, I think it was about a hundred and fifty yards to cover, maybe it was two hundred yards total, just to get to the soccer field was about a hundred yards. And the whole time these rocks are raining down. There was no command and control for some reason, the assumption was that we'd move in and meet on the soccer field. So, the company commander didn't really have any control over my platoon. I had an RTO that wasn't getting any commands sent. My RTO was right behind me in the formation and as the rocks come down my RTO was one of the first to get knocked out. He was knocked down and a former RTO picked up his radio and took over for him. The guys in the back of the platoon basically picked him up and dragged him along with us. As the rocks were pouring down the guys in the ranks were, you know, were basically hollering out in pain, but they're holding together, and we just kept moving forward, moving forward and moving forward. The mask on my helmet would get hit by rocks and the mask would concave in and hit me in the lip and fold back open. My mask was one of the few that didn't actually break. Body shields were breaking, face shields were breaking and we just kept moving and kept moving.

When we made it to the soccer field, I wasn't aware of it, I knew we were all hurt, but by the time we got there, two of my three squad leaders had broken bones and basically everybody in the platoon was fucked up. As we got there, because we were in a column I couldn't see behind me, but the company had started to break and run behind us. About the time we got to the soccer field word gets to me that everybody's running. I turn and look and sure enough, the company was scattering. Some of the guys in my platoon started asking, should we run, and I said no, stay the fuck together. The closest way out was the gate the Air Force was supposed to come through, but the Air Force didn't make it through the gate. I wheeled the platoon over, it wasn't really like, it over states to drill and ceremony, we held onto each other huddled together and stayed as turtled up as we could and we made our way to that gate. The gate was still closed because the demonstrators had moved a set of portable bleachers in front, but there was enough room that we could get our guys through the gap while protecting that small breach. Then we slowly got our guys out of the gap. When we finished getting through the gate, the platoon at that point was gone; the rioters kept coming after us and kinda pursued us, throwing rocks at us and everything. The confusion of going through the gap meant that, most of the guys were carrying the wounded to a casualty collection point that had been hastily put together. And the few of us that were left tried to do what we could to at least reform some kind of a line. At one point one of the rioters took over a deuce and a half and started to drive toward us to run us over. A quick thinking soldier got in a Humvee and tee-boned the deuce and a half, which stopped it, stalled it. That really was the end of their advance, then some folks that had brought tear gas started using it, which actually was, I don't know why they had it, but it was good that they did, since we weren't allowed. Somebody either violated orders or ignored it. The tear gas pretty much saved the day. So, they used tear gas and some of the tear gas got on us. But then the rioters went back to the camp. I went over to try and sort out the casualties. Of the twenty-five in the platoon, only eleven of my guys were, more or less, left standing. There were several I would have medevac'd out, but we had nobody so we couldn't. My platoon sergeant had a broken hand, but he wouldn't let me medevac him. The casualties were what you'd expect, one of my squad leaders had a broken leg, I think my other squad leader, I think my other two squad leaders had broken legs. One of my guys had a broken leg and a broken arm. It was reported that one of my guys was dead, but later on it was confirmed as a false report. They evac'd him right away with major head trauma. They told me he had died, but it turned out he hadn't. This whole time I was kinda in the zone, other than moments of snarkiness, or dark humor, I didn't really feel anything. It was just being in the moment. But, then I went over to check on one of my guys that was just covered in blood, he had multiple broken bones, he was lying there in this casualty collection point, which looked like something out of a civil war movie, you just had dozens and dozens of soldier, lying around in the grass with blood everywhere. I kneeled down to say something encouraging to him and I couldn't talk, I felt myself just break. I got up and just had to walk away and I just cried my eyes out. I kinda got my shit back together and went back there. We continued to wait for medevac. There was no plan for it, so it was all hasty.

About, it would have been, I don't know how many days, but about a week later we reconstituted what was left of the company. My platoon had the least guys after that and we went and retook, they didn't want us to retake the same camp, there were two riots going on simultaneously, they were smart and didn't want us to go back to the camp that hurt us, because they were afraid of discipline issues, which was legit. So, we went back and retook another camp aided by Rangers who were led by a guy named McChrystal. He was over there for a jungle warfare rotation. At that point me and my eleven men, our job was to sneak up and breach the fence line, and this time we did everything correctly. We did the breach at one in the morning or two in the morning; I can't remember what time it was, it was late at night. We completely ambushed the camp. We completely cut the breach, passed in my battalion; the Rangers went in through another breach. There basically wasn't even a fight. Same thing went on at the camp we'd been battered. That was the end of the riots. After that triple strength concertina went up everyone, there just weren't any issues after that. I carried a sidearm, we carried shotgun, there was just no more fucking around.

For years after that though, I questioned everything that I did. Why didn't I go to the battalion commander, why did I let my squad leader talk me out of it, would it have made any difference? Even marching into the camp, it was this bizarre situation where the platoon has been trained too well. If the platoon had been trained more poorly, if the discipline in the ranks when we marched in hadn't been as good, we actually wouldn't have suffered as many casualties. The men did what I ordered them to do, we kept moving until we realized we were basically alone and then we turned and ran out of there. But, even with that we maintained good discipline. But, you know, if anything, the good discipline caused us to suffer more casualties. So, just for me, I replayed it over and over and over and it was all the aspects of it. I felt betrayed by my chain of command, I felt like on so many levels that things were fucked up. We ended up closing the refugee camps and sending the Cubans back to Gitmo. There was this big ceremony where we were congratulated on a job well done, but it had all been a big disaster. It took until like April to close down the camps. We ended up closing them three or four months later, but it was all such a fiasco, that it really just haunted me for years. For me it later turned out that it was almost like Ahab losing his leg. For me there was just this open wound that wouldn't heal.

I went to Special Forces after that. For me, I needed to fight that again. Not literally the riots, but I kinda, it was somewhere between needing to, I guess the best way to put it, the essence of whatever I fought that day I needed to fight again. Part of it was I just needed to understand what the hell had happened, and part of it was I just needed to do it again. There was something I needed to understand about all of it. The reality was, as awful as December 8th had been, it also was, in an odd way, an amazing day. When you saw the bravery of your soldiers and you turn it around and see that we didn't break and run. Everybody broke and ran out, and these guys held together. There were parts of it I didn't feel bad about. There was this intensity to all of it that was kind of addicting. You don't know how you're going to respond in a situation like that, for me I was cold as a cucumber the whole time. It wasn't 'till basically it was done, that I went back into human mode and could come to grips with what had happened to everybody. But it was all stuff that I needed to see again, stuff I needed to understand; I needed to do it again.

So, I went into Special Forces, commanded my first A-Team and I went to the 5th Special Forces Group, commanded my first team, did a couple of deployment, but nothing terribly interesting going on. I asked for a second team, which for me, I didn't care about the career part of the military, for me it was I wanted to be in command for as long as I could. It was really in hopes of seeing that again. What's that old expression, 'Seeing the Elephant?' I took a second team in case something will go on in the world. I was at the end of the command of my second team, ODA-574, and the world was more or less at peace. I was a cadet during Panama and during Desert Storm. Somalia also happened while I was just in school. So, I basically had just missed everything and was at the end of my command. I had applied to the CIA and was hired. I was going to go to the farm and do all that stuff to become a case officer. Really that was it for me, one last deployment. I had to make peace with all that. I was flying to Kazakhstan and I remember sitting on the airplane, pondering Panama. I just had to make peace with the fact that it was done. There were no do-overs, whatever it was that I felt I needed to do, it wasn't going to happen. It was ok. At this point it had been seven years since Panama and I'd grown up quite a bit. So, I could live with that, so I could make peace, career is done, just move on, stop chasing that thing.

The deployment went well, we were training Kazaks to fight the Islamic movement of Uzbekistan. We were due to come back the third week of September; then 911 happened. I think a lot of people forget the rage and the anger, the legitimate rage and anger over the September 11th attacks. People talk as if we had an option of doing nothing. I won't go into the politics of the invasion of Iraq or the broader theory of a global war on terror, but as far as I was concerned we had to invade Afghanistan, we had to do what we did over there. It was pure luck that 574 and a handful of other teams were picked to spearhead the invasion of Afghanistan. And for me, it was kind of a switch had been thrown. Everything I saw in 1994 I was going to set right. I wasn't going to let that happen to my men again. We weren't going to fail a mission that way again, out of the stupidity of leadership. For my mindset, I was either given the best or worst mission that fed it. My mission was to go into southern Afghanistan to start a guerrilla war from scratch. We'd link up with a tribal leader, we'd work with him to start a resistance and we'd be on our own. All eyes were on the Northern Alliance; from the very beginning we were all but forgotten. 5th Group was focused on northern Afghanistan. My lone team was told to go into southern Afghanistan and our area of operations was the Pashtun tribal belt. We were independent, as I say we were largely ignored. Even when I was seeking guidance, I wouldn't be getting any responses. I mean it really was everything I joined Special Forces for, but also everything I needed after everything that happened in 1994. I couldn't have been captaining the ship any more thoroughly. I guess it's ironic to use a navy metaphor for an Army mission. I couldn't have been more in command of the mission, this was all on me and I wanted it to be.

From the get go the mission seemed like the odds were long against us. Afghanistan was the country where armies went to die. The

140

Mujahidin were legendary; I don't know why I had some much confidence. Part of it was I was very confident in my men, I was very confident in our training. I just felt like we could do all of this. I was going to take eleven men into southern Afghanistan and rely on people we didn't know to fight a campaign against an enemy we'd never met before. I'm 45 now and I look back on it, I don't know how as a 30 year old, I quite had the balls to do all of that. To me it was just, yeah, we can do it. We got on the ground on November 14th and three days later the few guerrillas we were able to raise were abandoning us. We're having to defend a whole city by ourselves from about a thousand Taliban that are coming after us. It was a completely dire moment that should have felt like the world was about to end. I had concerns, do I need to pull back, do I need to do this, it's not like I wasn't concerned about the tactical risks, but there was still this overwhelming confidence in our ability to fight this campaign. By the end of the day we'd destroyed the convoy, the Taliban were retreating to Kandahar, we'd saved the town. I felt like it was a reckoning for all the things I needed to fix from 1994. And for the next couple of weeks we were conducting this completely irregular air campaign where we're having to redefine the rules of engagement on the fly, we're having to follow up the Taliban in Kandahar, the city that we were there to take. Every bit of the campaign it felt like I was righting past wrongs; my own and just broader kind of professional wrongs that occurred in 1994. My men were winning; they were giving me the ability to win. As I said, we infiltrated on the 14th and by the beginning of December the Taliban were willing to surrender to the tribal leader that I was with, Hamid Karzai. It was already strongly hinted at that he would be the interim leader of the country.

We had kind of one final ground battle on December 3rd, it wasn't a big fight or anything, but we had to take a town called Shawali Kowt in order to kind of secure where we were just outside of Kandahar in order to secure the surrender of the Taliban. The fighting wasn't over, but it was getting close to being over and we had one last battle. We were able to fight and take Shawali Kowt. The first day of fighting on the third was kind of a crazy all day fight where we go in with just a couple dozen guys and chase out, probably, a hundred Taliban defending the town that didn't realize our numbers were so small. Once we held onto Shawali Kowt, one of our tribal leaders that came in late, tried to push into another town and he got chased out. We had this counter attack that basically surrounded my team in Shawali Kowt while most of our guerrillas ran and left us. We called this the Alamo. We were sitting on this hill while we watched the Taliban counterattack us, start to envelope us. I remember again there was just this feeling of exhilaration because we had them where we wanted them. We called in an AC-130 and we destroyed them; Shawali Kowt was held, the Taliban retreated. The whole campaign was textbook up to this point. And then the next day on the fourth, there was a bridge in the area, one bridge that went over a, mostly at this point, dry riverbed. The bridge was really a high-speed

142

avenue of approach. It wasn't perfect. These guys could get across the river on foot, but because of the vehicles and the tactics the Taliban employed, we really needed to hold, control the bridge. I didn't have the ability to control both sides of the bridge, I just wanted the north side of this bridge and this hill, it kinda just sat right there. There was this old fortress that had been on this hill that was really just walls and rubble. My team had growing pains; nobody had done a mission like this before. It was all sort of theory to do a guerrilla war like this. The attack to take the hill and the fort was another textbook Special Forces mission. Part of my guys, a split team they call it, was with an element of guerrillas controlling medium machine guns and light machine-guns, and my half of the team would be the ground force. My team sergeant with the light machine-guns and medium machine-guns would lay down suppressing fire and my half of the team with the ground force of guerrillas would peel up and physically seize the hill. It went great. The insurgent folks laid down fire, we took the hill. Some of the Taliban that were crossing the river felt like their flank was turned and they retreated back across the river. It felt like we finally secured Shawali Kowt, for whatever talks were to come and in theory the Taliban were going to face to face talks with Hamid in the coming days. As we were sitting on that hill, there was kinda of this moment, it was kind of the high water mark of the campaign where I just reflected on everything that got us to this point, and really it had just been, I felt like my own wounds had healed. But, in a bigger sense I was just so proud of what the men on the team had done.

We'd catch sporadic harassing fire, we just kept low, we were on a hill, you don't want to silhouette yourself, but we had these mud walls around us that you could get behind. Actually they were really big mud walls. This was, like I said, some kind of a fort once upon a time. Somebody shouts out that one of my guys had been shot. There was some confusion because we thought he could have been shot by one of our guerrillas, but it was pretty clear from the entry wound that yeah, somebody just got a lucky shot through, through this old break in a wall and it had hit my guy. At that point, I believe he was the first SF casualty to enemy fire, I mean literally in the War on Terror. I can't say that for certain. The round entered through his neck and exited through his upper back, didn't hit anything vital. He was pissed off, but he was fully mobile. When you have a bullet go completely through someone you worry about it. So, we medevac him. The absurdity of the invasion of Afghanistan, that we weren't aware of at the team level, especially my team since we were so removed from everybody else was a single SF guy getting shot like that sent shock waves up through the chain of command. The 5th Group commander ordered my team off the hill. We were basically ordered all the way back to Shawali Kowt; all over my guy Wes getting shot. That was the beginning of the cascade. We found ourselves back on top of the Alamo, the hill we had taken on the 3rd. Wes was going to be medevac'd that night. Headquarters folks were scheduled to come in late that night; they would be dropped off, Wes would get on. The headquarters folks were there to basically take over liaison with Karzai totally. A couple of headquarters folks had come in a week earlier, but they largely stayed out of my way and didn't really affect anything, but now a headquarters element bigger than my team was coming in. I knew that the war was basically over for my team at that point. I should say the campaign, not the war, because this headquarters was taking over. That made sense, because Hamid was going to be the interim leader of the country. Our job was done. Here we are, right at the end of such a successful campaign, and Wes gets shot, and we're getting bizarre orders from the highest echelons. It's what I feared from the beginning, it's what I was able to avoid, but now the big Army was here. There was a CIA element with my team and that night I sat with one of the CIA folks. He was the guy, part of Eagle's Claw, to rescue the Iranian hostages and had deployed pretty much everywhere imaginable. I remember looking at him and saying, 'Hey, it's December 4th, it's almost seven years to the day since basically my whole platoon was wounded in these riots. I guess I'm some kind of a widow maker.' He said, 'Wes will be fine, it could have been a lot worse. We're at war, what would you expect would happen? But, I wouldn't tell anybody else that story.' I laughed, and said, 'Yeah, I know.'

The next morning, the morning of December 5th, Wes was safely medevac'd out and the headquarters came out and basically got up on the hill with us. I had friends on the headquarters, there was nothing personal between me and them, the issue was more the professional side of why am I being routed off the hill by somebody that's hundreds of miles away. When the headquarters got up on the hill they began directing air strikes against this ridgeline, basically across the river and across the bridge from us. There was nothing there; it didn't make any sense. I went over to the S3 and he said there were Taliban on the ridge. I knew there weren't. I even think that he knew there weren't. They wanted to get in some airstrikes before the so-called war, was over. I was pissed off. They said we want you to go retake that hill over there and I want you to brief one of my guys on your plan. I said, 'We did the live fire yesterday so we're ready to brief it whenever you want.' I was just livid. I walked back over. Red, one of his assistants, who's a friend of mine, and started talking to him about what happened yesterday, us getting pulled off the hill and now we're being ordered to retake the hill. The assistant 3, was a guy named Dennis, who I'd known since the Infantry Officer's Basic Course, so we talked for a little bit and then one of the Tactical Air Controllers who'd come in with the headquarters who was directing airstrikes in combat for the first time, he used a Viper incorrectly. He had it set so the grid coordinates would be buffered and he didn't realize it. To test this device, he had lazed at his feet to confirm there was a grid in there and then he lazed the target and then when he read the grid coordinate, he didn't realize he was reading the grid coordinate at his feet. He called in a two thousand pound JDAM and it came in and hit the forward edge of the hill. The casualties were catastrophic. Everyone on my team was wounded. Jefferson Davis, the team sergeant was killed, Dan Petithory the commo sergeant was killed. A friend of mine on the headquarters, named Cody Prosser was killed and we had, people have come up with different numbers for the wounded, but we had about a hundred wounded. And then among my Afghans, there's always been different numbers of dead. I thought thirty. One of the CIA guys that had stayed behind told me that it was more like fifty. We'll never know because of the complete carnage. The only reason we didn't all die was that the two-thousand-pounder was set to penetrate, otherwise it would have been a surface detonation and we all would have died. All the guerillas were massed on the hill watching the show so everybody was in a compact little area when the two thousand pound bomb hit. That's why the casualties were so bad as it was. At that point we went into a mass casualty crisis mode. Triaging, keeping people alive, doing everything we can. Dennis the assistant S3 I told you about, he was incredible. We all get medical training but he did an amazing job working on the casualties. We also had several people with more formal training, but the reason I highlight Dennis was that when the casualties were more or less stabilized there was an ongoing period, I looked at Dennis and reminded him of the last time we saw each other, and that was in Panama. He was deployed from the 101st to help keep refugees out after we'd been so thoroughly beat up on December 8th. Here we were again, seven years almost to the day, and here I am with Dennis who came in seven years earlier to help me, and here he was helping me out again with all these casualties.

Initially we were excited because the Marines had come into Rhino and were, and I don't know how far they were away, I was told they were forty-five minutes away by helicopter, and we were told that the Marines would come in and get us. But, then Mattis refused to launch his helicopters for a medevac, claiming he didn't understand the tactical situation, he didn't want to take the risk. Which would be ironic later in the invasion of Iraq when he relieved a battalion commander for being too hesitant in combat. The folks that ended up saving us that day were from AFSOC. We'd been working with them to plan the mission, and they had launched a pair of MH-53s to come get us. The MH-53s, they had a three hour flight to get to us, those old birds, they flew basically past Rhino to get to us, then with almost no fuel left, dropped us at Rhino. At that point Mattis, finally decided to send medevac and was able to get the rest of our casualties out. That was the end of the campaign for me and my men. We got evacuated to Oman initially, then flown on to Landstahl, Germany. My guys left ahead of me because I had to officially ID Dan's remains. JD was right under the blast so identification of his remains had to be by DNA. I stayed back, officially ID'ed Dan and escorted Dan's body to Germany. Walking off the plane in Germany, I had gotten a haircut and a fresh uniform from the Air Force folks from the MASH unit there so I could escort Dan's body with dignity. At least I was cleaned up, but the only boots that could fit me were the ones I was wearing in Afghanistan and they still had gore on them. So, here I am, I'm taking Dan's body to Germany and a well meaning public affairs officer comes up to me and says SOCOM would really like me to do a press conference because the American public thinks the invasion is going poorly and we need them to know what's going on. My eardrums were blown out; I had some shrapnel in me, nothing serious. The thing about Panama that pissed me off was you had a massive horrible chaotic event that nobody ever heard of. To this day, nobody's ever heard of the riots in Panama. Back in '94 people were still talking about Somalia. It was as if it didn't happen. I wasn't going to let what happened to my men get covered up. For me, it was with a vengeance. Ok, I'll do a press conference. I basically got up there and said I wasn't going to focus on how they died, I was going to tell you about the incredible mission and what they did on the mission. I unfortunately got my tagline. Me and my folks will always be the team that was hit by the JDAM. We're also always going to be the team that brought the future president of Afghanistan into the country. To this day, if anyone wants me to tell the story, I'll tell it because I'm not going to let the truth of what happened get covered up or forgotten. Now, in looking back on all of that, as I say, it's sort of Moby Dick, only I didn't have to die with the whale. I don't know if that means that the fates were kinder to me, or I didn't deserve so bad a fate, or if it would have been kinder if I had died that day instead of men. I mean all of it haunts me, just in a different way.

So, December 8ᵗʰ 1994 marched into camps in Panama and all my men were wounded. December 5ᵗʰ 2001 took my men into Afghanistan and all my men were wounded and two of them were killed. In Panama I had no control over anything. Afghanistan, I had control until I didn't have control anymore and it was essentially the same result. So, I guess people can take any lessons they want from it. It's war, when you go to war, people die; but hopefully it's for a good reason. And that's my war story."

Jason recently retired from the US Army, from a position of great responsibility, working in Washington DC. Recently married, he's enjoying a new career and writing.

****

Vet: *"Anthony"*
Setting: *My house, sitting at the poker table in my bar/rec room.*
Drinks: *Anthony and I were alternating between Heineken and Warsteiner Dunkel. We also had a bottle of Carnivore Red Wine Anthony brought for dinner.*

Story: "Cheers, thanks for the opportunity to do this, this is cool. I never really told the story, not this way in its entirety. I've been wanting to do this for a long time, so I can kinda capture it. You're busy, you go through life, you're busy, you capture pieces of it and sometimes I think it's important to put it all in its entirety and go forth. And like we talked about earlier, I don't think this is a story about me, I had a front row seat, I'm a character in it, but it's about a lot of other people as well. Two people in particular, BV and BL, two of my very first supervisors were both positive examples.

You have this young Airman, coming into the Air Force, whose initial plans were to come in for four years, gain a skill, get money for college and go back out into the civilian world and do great things. But, they were part of developing the Airmanship in me and causing the light bulb to come on. One example, BV in particular, I remember when we were out on the range one night; I came in thinking that nobody was in the office right? And he's still there. He's our supervisor, he's our leader, but he's still there. I'm like, 'What are you still doing here? Why are you here?' It just so happened that he lived about an hour and a half from the office. He said to me, 'We still have men out on the range, can't go home until they come in.' I thought at that time, wow, I want to be like that guy when I grow up. It gets better because I'm thinking to myself, he lives an hour and a half away, he's going to get home at twelve thirty, one O'clock, fall asleep, and we do PT pretty early, so he'll probably come in late tomorrow. But no, I show up for PT and he's already there ready to go. He went home probably got about three hours of sleep, got back in his car and came back. Talk about somebody who was leading by example every single day. These are the first two supervisors who showed me what right looked like. That's basically what they did. At the same time who I'll call peers, based on rank right? Guys like CG, KH, and another guy I'll call Jimbo. You know the difference between good and great right? Great people have the ability to make people around them better than they ever would have been otherwise. These three guys, I'll tell they're the reason I'm at where I'm at today. The reason I was able to be successful in different events throughout my career. Everything they did, either purposeful, or by nature of how they are, it was the competitive nature make their buddies better, to make me better. It was just that helping hand when you needed that helping hand. When you didn't get it right, they never ridiculed you or tried to reduce you down, they tried to lift you back up. They would give you another way, you know? Those five people that were in my career, in my life in those first few formative years, if you will, were able to enable me to get other opportunities. As I focused in on being the best that I could be at my craft, which was being a enlisted Terminal Attack Controller, that's all we did, how do we get better. The time I had with those individuals, whether it was a supervisor showing me what right looked like, or peers that invested in me and helped me and helped make me who I was at the time, and quite frankly, who I am today. All that stuff has carried on and led to new opportunities and new assignments and opportunities to work with Special Operators in the Army community. Specifically, working with the Rangers. It was at a time in the late '90s, we weren't extremely busy, so you continue down that path and do a lot of exercises where you were preparing, preparing, preparing, and it was at that time when I move to the Rangers, that I had a new group of teammates, peers, that also influenced who I am today. LT, CW, KDV, Manny, another CG, I'll call him CG II, great teammates, warrior mindset, just trying to be better at our craft then anyone in our career field; that was our total focus. Shoot, move, communicate; we tried to be the experts at all of it. I remember this one time in one week; we went to shoot with a box of ammo. We shot all day long, we took a break and we shot into the night, every position you could think of we did, trying to hone our skills. The next day we went and jumped out of helicopters, five different jumps. The next day we went to the bombing range and we worked CAS for the entire day. As a TACP, what better week could you have, right? We do all of that in one week. While we were honing our skills and honing our craft, time ticks on and eventually we get to September of 2001, the World Trade Center, the Pentagon, Pennsylvania, the world changes for everybody. At the time, when it comes to going to war, you're at the best place at the best time, right? Because you know you're going to be in the thick of it, and you're around some of the most phenomenal human beings on the face of the earth. The person to your left and your right, you don't have to worry about whether they've got your back. You don't have to worry if they have to shoot straight, or whether they're going to do their job when it's time. It was just a phenomenal place to be at the time. Eventually, we got opportunities to go. Multiple opportunities. We were going for short periods of time, but multiple times a year.

On about the fifth trip, the part of this story that's, 'there I was.' I want to highlight, it was a short discussion we just talked about, but I want to highlight all of the things that happened up to this point, all of the people that contributed to enabling me going to be successful, on those trips. I often tell people, 'Nobody gets here alone.' These people are the people that helped me get to where I was. So, multiple trips, multiple big events, but I come to one that was particularly significant, at least for me, because it ended in a helicopter ride and an airplane ride to a hospital and multiple surgeries and recoveries from significant wounds. So, on my fifth combat tour, this one happens to be in support of Operation Enduring Freedom, we're hanging out on the border of Pakistan and Afghanistan.

We begin movement under the cover of darkness and we get ambushed, small arms fire, RPGs fly over the lead vehicle and we start receiving small arms fire. I'm sitting in the back of a Humvee, I turn to return fire, I put my weapon on 'fire' and an RPG explodes over my head. It shoves me down to the back of the Humvee that I'm sitting in. I jump down, peel off to my right, away from enemy fire at this point to try and get my wits about me, and then I'm pulling security on that side of our formation, so that nobody from the backside is going to get us. My NVGs are inop at this time, I'm trying to fix those, then all of a sudden the left side of my body feels like it's on fire. From my left side of my face to my neck, my shoulder, my left arm, all feels like it's on fire. Obviously, I could look down and see that it's not. My left eyelid is completely shut; I couldn't even pry it open if I wanted to. At this point I realize something's not right. I'm trying to check everything out, and I kinda lose focus on pulling security. A buddy of mine comes over and starts checking me over and says, 'Hey, you just got a couple scratches on your face, no big deal, it's going to be ok.' About forty-five minutes later we're on a helicopter, take an initial stop to get initial treatment. There were three other Rangers with me who took the trip. We moved on to a more stabilizing location and then eventually on to a hospital in Europe for sustainment care. In about a week I was back in the United States, in San Antonio, at Lackland for my care.

Essentially what had happened, an RPG had exploded over my head, took shrapnel to the left side of my face, had about a two inch gash in my neck, a golf ball sized hole and a softball sized hole in my shoulder and arm, and a gunshot wound, graze to my left arm and a dozen or so smaller flesh wounds if you will, shrapnel wounds, to the left side of my body. Which led to them taking my left eye out, replacing it with a prosthetic and then back on to home about a month after all this happened to begin the recovery process and find the new normal. And figure out what's next. I had been in the Air Force for about ten years at the time and I knew, lying on the battlefield that I wasn't done yet. I didn't know what was in store in the future but I knew that I wasn't done contributing and serving, I just didn't know what that looked like yet.

After we come back from getting fixed up and we begin the recovery process we start talking with the medical providers and start doing medical waivers and at the same time I'm going through the medical evaluation board, physical evaluation board where they're trying to determine if I can stay in the Air Force; can I still serve. Luckily, with the help of General Hornburg, who was the ACC commander at the time, he basically pushed my MEB and PEB in about three weeks. The Air Force came back and said, you can stay in the Air Force, you can continue to serve, no restrictions. And then we began the medical waiver side of it, can I continue to jump, static line or free fall, continue to control air, continue to be a TACP. The great team of docs put a lot of effort into this, pushed the package up, but it came back really quickly. The medical community said, they're kinda looking at it by the black and white AFI. The AFI says you don't have a left eye, you can't serve in this role, you have to have depth perception, you can't jump out of airplanes, so, basically no to everything. About the time that was coming back I was making a move to the staff to continue to work, obviously I couldn't stay where I was at, I had to make room, I didn't have the full capacity to fight in combat, so I went to the staff in a training role, a training manager role, while we figured out what was next.

Actually, my very first supervisor, who I spoke about before, BV, happened to now be on the staff and became my supervisor again. With his vast experience, he knew there were waivers to everything, there are ways to overcome this medical 'no.' He and I guy by the name of KG, went to work on this exception to policy package. They worked on that, they continued to have discussions with leaders. Once I heard BV talk about, 'The guy lost his eye, not his brain.' They were constantly my advocates to continue to serve, to continue to play a role in the TACP community. It took a little while; it took about eight months. The waiver that they worked, they pushed through the Air Force, through Air Combat Command all the way to Headquarters Air Force. It came back and it had some stipulations. I could continue to jump, static line only, no military free fall. I couldn't control air anymore, because I didn't have any depth perception, one of the requirements for being a controller, you have to have depth perception. I could stay in the career field, if I proved that I could do every task required of a 1C4, a TACP. So, I couldn't free fall, couldn't be a controller and I couldn't deploy – no longer could I deploy to combat.

At the time I remember thinking to myself, Ok, at least there's an opportunity. At least there's a chance to continue to serve in this community in what I've been doing. And I could contribute in some way. I went to work and had a three-day eval, where I had to prove to an evaluator that I could do every task required of a TACP. I got through that three-day evaluation, passed everything and got the thumbs up from the senior evaluator from higher headquarters. The very next day, BV asked me if I wanted to deploy. I was kinda shaking my head, 'Did you read the same waiver I read? Yeah, I'd like to deploy but my waiver said that I can't. It's not one of the things they're going to allow me to do.' BV had a way with things and said, 'Yeah, yeah, yeah, yeah... don't worry about that.' I said, 'Ok, I do want to deploy, but before I tell you yes, I'm all in, I need to go home and I need to talk to somebody, because I wasn't on the other end of that phone call that I had to make about two years ago and I need to make sure she's ok with it.' And so, that night I went home, I asked my wife to sit down, 'I need you to sit down,' we were sitting at the dinner table, she was on one corner, I was on the other corner and I said, 'I just need to ask you a question. No matter what you say, I'm ok with it.' And I just said, 'I want to go back,' and she just said, 'Ok.' That was the extent of the conversation. A month later I was in Iraq, serving obviously in a different role, as a squadron superintendent at the time. I was back in the fight, contributing in my own way.

I come back from that and one of the things BV wanted me to do, he wanted me to continue down the normal path of a TACP, which went that I had to go lead guys that were going to do things that I couldn't do anymore. That kinda scared me. I was asking guys to do things in combat that the Air Force would not allow me to do, put themselves in harm's way while I was sitting back in a staff somewhere coordinating the assets that they needed or doing whatever it was they needed me to do for them. I was really resistant to the idea of going to do that. Very early on as a very young NCO BV said, 'Nope, you're going to do this, you're going to be an Ops Supt of a squadron.' I was really young, for this job. My experiences at this point, I'd spent a lot of time in this small team, special operator type environment, so at the same time I had missed some things that would have helped me, would have made it easier to be successful in that role.

I'll tell you, the next year and a half was kind of an uphill climb. I was working hard, spending a lot of hours. Everyday I would ask myself did I do enough today for the men and women of the organization? Some days I would walk out and I'd say, 'Yeah, I think so.' But there were other days and I'd walk out and said, 'Maybe not. Maybe I didn't have the capability to do it. I didn't have the knowledge or experience up to that point, because I was relatively young.' To kinda back up a little bit, I'll tell you about KG. KG was a commander, and that wasn't the first time I worked with KG either. I worked with KG in that small Ranger team previously as well. One of the things that he did; commanders have changes of command, and it's the one time I think, toward the end of command it can, a little bit be about you. You can use that time, cherish that time and make it a little bit about you. But that's not what he did. He used that last opportunity to talk about me and he was basically soliciting his boss to allow me to deploy again. Took something that was supposed to be about him, and made it about somebody else. Part of the reason I had the opportunity to deploy again. BV was once again telling people over and over again, literally, argue with people, I lost my eye not my brain and I still had capacity. There's no way I'd be where I am today without those two, specifically for me.

We continue on with the Ops Supt job to a Squadron Supt job in a squadron. In my opinion there is no great job, and this just wasn't any squadron, you know? I mean they are all awesome; every single one of them, but one of them is somewhat unique. I had the opportunity to be the Squadron Supt of that unique squadron, that's well known throughout our community. Once again surrounded by just some phenomenal human beings going to do great things for our country, every single day. The next step is Senior NCO Academy, then Group Chief and deploying again; working with guys like FM.

I remember distinctly our conversation when I left the Group. When I had left the Group to go to the Squadron, because you had recently come off of being the commander there and just, I remember the confidence you had in me going into that role. There was you, Col S., who had replaced KG, BV and it just seemed like you guys had all the confidence in me when I wasn't sure I could do what you were asking me to do. I just trusted that you guys knew. I went and did the very best I could. Obviously from the very beginning it was like building a foundation, then built walls, then built rooms, then built a roof and everything just built on each other that created more opportunity. One thing just led to another thing. I guess it's not that awkward, it just feels awkward right? I mean that's how life happens, but when you look back at it in its entirety it's like wow, what an experience, what an opportunity to serve with, serve side by side with the people I had the opportunity to serve side by side with, like I said, there were great leaders, great operators, great, phenomenal human beings. I'm here where I'm at today, I mean I had successes because of every single one of them that I talked about; invested into me.

Some days I wonder if I invested as much into them as they did into me, and I can only hope the answer to that is yes. I know that nobody gets to where they're at alone and I surely did not get here all by myself.

Anthony continues to serve and excel in Senior Enlisted positions throughout the Air Force.

****

Vet: *"El Cid"*
Setting: *Park Lane Pub, Peninsula Town Center, Hampton, VA*
Drinks: *El Cid had a Smithwicks Ale, I had a cup of coffee.*

Story: "This was during Operation ANACONDA, I showed up at Bagram on 18 March 2002. I had gotten to Jacobabad on the 4th, left there on the 12th, got back to Al Jaber on the 13th and did planning, packing and loading from 14-16 March. So, on 18 March we're building a camp. Me and a Sergeant are building a slit trench. Muck Brown was a legendary A-10 pilot and a close and longtime friend of mine. His son, an Army Specialist fighting in Op Anaconda, walks up to me. I'm just wearing desert camouflage pants, he says, 'I'm looking for the A-10 commander.' I said, how can I help you specialist? He says, 'My dad says to find you and tell you my story.' I ask him, what are you supposed to tell me? He says, 'On 5 March I was getting mortared and I thought I was going to die. An A-10 showed up and BRRRTTTT... killed the mortar.' I wasn't actually the one flying that sortie, it was AK that scraped those mortars off and saved their lives. I had held that specialist, my good friend's son, in my arms when he was a baby. I told Specialist Brown that and me and Muck drank to that event when I saw him when I got back home.

El Cid led the contingent of A-10s to forward deploy in support of Operation Anaconda. That awesome firepower and infusion of airborne Forward Air Controllers helped ensure victory. El Cid went on to hold several high visibility and important senior positions within the Air Force before retiring. He remains key heavy hitter in the Joint community.

Operation Iraqi Freedom
20 March 2003 – December 2011

The operation began with the "Shock and Awe" air campaign that lasted three days then the ground invasion began. The 3rd Infantry Division moved westward then north and the 1st Marine Expeditionary Force moved eastward then north. The UK 1st Armored Division moved north through the eastern marshland. 3rd ID captured Baghdad Airport, the Marines fought their way to the eastern side of Baghdad. The 101st had captured the Karbala gap, enabling the approaches to Baghdad. Baghdad fell on 9 April and Sadam Hussein's regime fell. Although the invasion was very successful the follow on political decisions had strategic impacts that would reverberate for years to come. The insurgency started within a few short months.

Over four tours, starting with the invasion, I experienced the transformation of the country and the evolution of combat in response to that evolution. IEDs, rockets, booby traps, ambushes, snipers, stability and sustainment, etc. We would assault and fight to regain cities that were supposedly liberated in 2003. We enabled elections, we tried and then we left. Civil war. And now we're back. From 2003 – 2014, 4,491 US service members were killed. Estimates of the Iraqi dead vary widely, but may be in the hundreds of thousands.

Air Support Operations Center, Outskirts of Baghdad

Vet: *"Conan"*
Setting: *By the pool at Mike B's house in Northern Virginia, the day after the premier of RANGE 15, (we can play this up here and pitch/leverage the movie, etc, or just mention it in passing at this point – since by time the book is published it will be an international mega-hit).*
Drinks: *Conan and I were both having ice cold Pacificos.*

Story: "I've told this story before, not sure where to start. I was the only Air Guard guy to jump into Iraq. We had a whole group of guys that were supposed to be part of that, but the active duty guys kinda stuck it to them and said, 'No, not now, we're going to have our E-3's and E-4's, non-JTACs, jump in because we can't have all you guys go in the first wave right? What if everybody dies?' Shut up. So, how I got involved in this, let me back up a little further. It's the Guard right, so, I had to go in for something and there were a couple of guys that were on the hook to do this from the 116th and one of them kinda limping a little bit when he walked in. So I said, 'What's up?' He says, 'I was ruck marching this morning and stepped off the pavement and kinda rolled my ankle.' I was like, 'Whoa, man, that's not good. You don't want to try and jump on that.' He said, 'Whaddya mean?' I said, 'You know, you hit the DZ and hurt that ankle even more and they're gonna have to leave ya.' He said, 'Leave me?' I said, 'Yeah...well, good luck.' Well I was there for a few hours, doing some paperwork or something, anyway, was there for a few hours and by the time I left he had a very pronounced limp (Conan looked sideways at me while saying that). He was trying to get off of the deployment. The commander, even before I left says, 'Hey, this guy is potentially hurt, we're going to send him over to get x-rays, but, is there any chance you're interested in going?' I said, 'Sure, I'll go, no problem – you jumping into Iraq? Sure, yeah, no problem. As a matter of fact, it's probably just safe to take him off now because that's not going to heal up.' Well, I don't think he was that hurt, but he allowed himself to get talked out of it, and got removed. So, we had a series of phone calls. I seemed to be the only Guard guy on these calls over the STU and in them I was told I was the only one jumping. So, I knew, even before I went over to Italy to join up with the guys, that I was jumping, that's it. Well, all the other Guard guys that were pulled in for this to augment, they were all told they were jumping.

We got there, the war itself had just kicked off, the big Shock and Awe was going on. We were sitting in Vicenza with the detachment of 4th ASOG, or something, I don't remember. So, we were just sitting there watching the news. Of course, it's rolling twenty four hours a day, we're seeing strikes going and we also see when the guy rolled the grenades into the TOC and Major Stone was killed. So, all that's coming right there, we're watching it real time on the news. But, the Army is dead set on doing this jump. We find out that 10th Group has already secured the DZ with the Peshmerga. And I do think the reason we actually jumped was to keep Turkey out, because Turkey had a couple Battalions on the border ready to go and start killing Kurds. But, under the cover of darkness a thousand barrel-chested freedom fighters jump in. We had all the rehearsals and everything there on the parade field. At the end of it, the 173rd Airborne Sergeant Major gets up and he's giving his little pep talk and HooAh, HooAh speech then says, 'Do we have any questions?' I raise my hand. I'm in modified uniform with pockets sewn on my sleeves, so he goes, 'Oh, Air Force, what do ya got Air Force?' So, I asked the question, 'Since 10th Group already secured the airfield why aren't just flying in and landing and getting everybody there in about an hour?' It was like I asked to anally rape his mom while pouring sugar in his gas tank. Well the collective breath of the whole 173th was (makes a gasping sound) and I had to leave the parade field pretty quickly, or I was gonna get lynched. 'Next question! We're fucking jumping!' I said, 'Ok Sergeant Major, thanks, good talk.'

We had to go down to Aviano and they actually stopped transatlantic transport flights to get enough C-17s to do this jump. We're sitting there at Aviano, we're going through sustained and all that and I asked the question, 'So, the heavies are going in first, right?' and they were like, 'Of course.' I asked, 'How are they marked?' They said, 'Chem sticks.' I said, 'Great, what color?' They said, 'IR dummy!' and I came back with, 'Oh yeah, we can't jump with nods, it's a static line jump. How do we see them?' There was a long pause, 'Uhhh...' I'm like, 'Ok, awesome.' And we did have people slamming into ISU-90s, there were significant, uh, casualties sounds a bit dramatic, but, and actually I got fucked up to, but that comes later. The entire airfield is now dedicated to this airborne operation. A thousand troops, all our gear, laid out by chocks and we get everything squared away. So, they're going to have a steak and lobster feast, so I was like, 'Ok, let's go boys...' Well, these guys stop us and say, 'Who are these guys?' and I tell them that these are my troops. I was acting as an EBALO, which, that's another story right – what a terrible idea that was. So anyway, I say, 'Why can't my guys go get dinner?' They say, 'They can have dinner, they just can't have the steak and lobster.' I said, 'Why not?' and the answer was, 'They're not on the manifest.' So, I said, 'They're going to war,' he says back, 'Yeah, but they're not jumping. They're going on day two.' So, I look at the guys and they're pissed.

They're not jumping anyway and now they're more pissed because they're getting treated like that. So, we went to Burger King and had a Double Whopper and Cheese eating contest, to see who could eat it in the fewest bites. I won; I ate it in three bites.

We ended up sleeping on our gear that night and then we're getting up and then we're doing it. They had briefed that we were jumping at 1200 feet, that's a pay jump. They issued us reserves, right? So, I already asked my question, I already highlighted myself. Hmm, 1200 feet, we've got reserves, this is not, jumping into Normandy; this is a PR show. Now, the next day, I think it was the 26th of March is when we jumped in; we have to chute up, get inspected and sit on the plane forever. So, it's just me. They've got this private running around and he comes up to me and says, 'What size chute do you need?' I said, 'I need a six.' He says, 'Okay!' and he runs off. There aren't any sixes; the chute sizes only go up to five. But, the longer I'm not wearing that, the happier I am. So, he comes back and says, 'I can only get a five.' Well, I asked him, 'Does it have the triple canopy?' He say, 'Whadya mean?' Well, I said, 'I'm 300 pounds, with the kit and everything else, I'm close to 500 pounds, I need more than one canopy.' So, he says, 'Geez, I don't know sergeant,' then off he goes. Now I can see him, and he's getting his ass chewed. He's down there and he's pointing back at me, and this guys is putting his finger in his chest, so now it's time to stop fucking with the private. So, we get chuted up, we get on the flight, sitting there, take off and there's this kid sitting right across from me, this Lieutenant, this was his cherry blast. Right, so everyone's telling him, that's a case of beer. And he's like, 'Seriously?' and we said, 'Yes. First time to war?' we asked him, 'Yes,' he said, so, of course, 'That's another case of beer.' And there were a few of us, I had just gotten back from Afghanistan and I'd been home for about five months when this started happening. So, I know we're not jumping into anything dangerous, right?, so, no big deal. But, there are some guys on this flight that were, 'This is war!' and I was like, 'Ehh, not really, the war's a bit south from where we're jumping. But, no problem, we'll find it.' But, unbeknownst to us, it had snowed about an hour before we actually jumped in.

So, there was cloud cover that pushed our ceiling down and they actually put us out...I was chock three, left door, so that plane put us out about 700 feet. Would have been good to know that, right? So, I fall quickly, I achieve terminal velocity rapidly, right? So, there's cloud cover, they'd cut the power to the town nearby, there's no ambient light, so you can't really see the horizon, but you can look down and you can see the airstrip. I'm definitely not landing on that, right? To the right of it, it looks like a plowed field, and it was. That was the only thing that saved me. Because, as I'm looking at it, and trying to get the horizon, I reach over to release my ruck and I hit the ground. It was left foot – face – unscheduled nap. There were five minutes spacings between chocks. When I came to, or woke up, my next conscious thought was, there are planes coming overhead. I gotta get off the DZ. I figured I kicked up this massive divot, because I felt this big pack of mud, so I started kicking away from it; it was actually my ruck. I didn't have a helmet; it had gotten smashed and thrown off, all the webbing torn out. I have a concussion, I hurt my head – the only thing that saved me was that plowed field. So, that was the good and the bad. I don't know if you heard about the mud that we had to deal with in the north. Well, that's what I landed in and well, that stuff is like cement. It would just pancake around your boots and instead of like snowshoes, helping you walk on it, it made it heavier, and that was miserable. But, I'm looking up and now I can see canopies opening and I don't want someone to land on me. But, everything is slow – just can't get in gear. I'm trying to put my weapon in service, trying to get the radio going to make comms, tell them I'm hurt, can't find my helmet. I think I told them three times I was hurt, because the last time, they responded back, 'We know...we got it...' It was just a miserable night, it was cold, it was wet, people are showing up to the rally point with no gear, no weapons. You ask them at first, 'Where's your stuff,' and they respond, 'Uh, it burned in,' and, it's credible, at night, everybody hit hard and people were put wide, some were put short. So, what they told us was there were no actions for towed jumpers. Sorry, man, we'll pull you back in when we get to Aviano. At the far end of the DZ were mountains, so they had to get to 5000 feet, right now. So, if you were towed, you're screwed. What's not known was there were a lot of people who didn't get out of the plane. There were a couple of mortar men; they were struggling with the base plates.

The biggest problem was, Turkey hadn't let us come in, or they weren't going to let us overfly initially, but then they did, but we had to fly at 35,000 feet, until we hit Iraqi airspace. Then we had to go from 35,000 feet to jump altitude. We're all standing ready to jump all facing the rear of the plane ready to go. Coming from 35 to roughly 1000 feet, the planes like this right? (Conan, sticks his hand out and dramatically tilts his fingers toward the ground). You're walking up hill to get out the door. Another thing that was really messed up, most of the guys in the 173rd, had never jumped the C-17. They had 130s all the time, so that extra step you had to take to get out the door of the C-17, they weren't doing it, and they were gumming guys up. So, instead of pass off-step-out, it's pass off-step-step-out, so they're just gumming up the doorway. I'm shoving; like, 'Get the fuck out the door,' you know, let's go. So, some people didn't make it. Actually it was probably better for them. We finally get this hodgepodge of people on the ground, everybody's covered in mud and everyone's got various states of missing gear, weapons, whatever. We get to the far end of the airfield and the Kurds have this tent set up, they're serving us Chai, to take the cold off, it's surreal. They had to move, they had DAPS aircraft on the airfield, they had to move them away to make sure they didn't get crushed by the heavies and us jumping. This was total PR. The next morning, they say that I clearly had my bell rung, so they get this SF medic, who is truly fucked up, his foot is turned around, he's using his M4 as a crutch and he does the horizontal nystagmus test and says, 'Yep, you've got a concussion,' like no shit, I know that, and then says, 'Don't let him go to sleep 'cause he's got a head injury.' I ask, 'So what about can I get something for my hip?' He's says, 'No, you've got a head injury.' Well, I said, 'You can't give me anything for my head, you can't give me anything for my hip?' And the medic says, 'Yeah, good luck.' So, like Bubba Gump, I'm leaning back to back with my radio guy maintaining radio watch all night. Then the next morning the sun starts coming up and it's gonna be another cold dreary day – and you can see dotted all over the landscape, all this gear. And you know what happened, and my ruck was 141 pounds, we were jumping heavy, they just hit the ground and said, 'Ah fuck it.' Nobody's shooting at them, no danger. We sat there for weeks waiting on the Herc and Merc to come down out of Germany with tanks; then we were going to roll up those pesky Iraqis. That jump itself was a debacle. The only reason they did it was CNN would cover it and Turkey would not roll over the border; that was it. We got mustard stains for it, which was great, but it kinda loses something when people want to talk tough about the jump, I just say, 'I was there, nobody was shooting at you.' You know, some guys got put out in the town, some went long, short, but that's a different story, that's hairy. But, when I come out and there's the PI, I'm going to hit it, not a lot of drift with me. So, that's it the story of moving the herd."

Conan was the only Air National Guardsman to make the jump. When he wasn't downrange he was a Washington State Trooper, a Detective and SWAT leader. The concussion he sustained on that jump absolutely affected his career path decision. While responding to a SWAT call, standing at the ready in the freezing rain for hours he realized he needed to be doing something else. He'd spent a lot of time practicing being miserable and figured there's gotta be something that might not be as taxing on his body. He came off that call, went off duty, downed three tall shots of Jameson's and decided he was going to go to law school. Today he's a lawyer specializing in International Business Law and expeditionary law.

****

Vet: *"Josh"*
Setting: *Salsa and Beers Restaurant, Spring Lake, NC, just outside of Fort Bragg. I was at Fort Bragg for an exercise and Josh drove up from his home in South Carolina to see me and help me with a problem. I had cancer. Josh being a faithful man and a good friend wanted to pray over me. But, we were going to have some Mexican food first.*
Drinks: *We both had water.*

Story: "Alright, well, my story starts out in Afghanistan. It was the Fall of 2002, Anaconda and all that had already happened and in those days there were no roadside bombs, improvised explosive devices and all that. We just went out looking for the bad guys, and when we found 'em, we'd engage 'em, and that's just kinda what we did and we ruled the country. We traveled no smaller than company sized units and being the 82d Airborne, we had big firepower and so we kinda ruled Afghanistan. Anywhere we'd go we'd get in little skirmishes but they wouldn't last long because we had a lot of firepower.

Anyway, in early 2003 they started talking about us going into Iraq to overthrow Saddam and his regime, the Bath party, that kinda stuff. So, I was set to redeploy in the Spring of 2003. I was set to come home and started thinking, well, if this thing happens in Iraq, I'm gonna miss it. So, I call back to Fort Bragg and talked to my commander at the time and said, 'Hey what's going on in Iraq, is there gonna be a war over there?' And he said, 'Yeah, it looks like it.' So, I said, 'Well if I deploy, I'll be redeploying while you guys are deploying over to Iraq, and I'm gonna miss out on that.' So, he says, 'Well, why don't you stay right where you're at in Afghanistan and we'll see what develops in Iraq and we'll go from there.' So, anyway, I stayed in Afghanistan for a few more months, communicating with my commander the whole time. Then finally, he says, 'Well, it looks like we're gonna do something in Iraq, the 82d's on their way over there, why don't you try and make your way from Afghanistan over to Iraq and meet up with us over there?' So, I said, 'Ok, sounds good.' So, it's not hard to get a flight, so I flew from Afghanistan to Kuwait and found where we were setting up, where the 82d set up camp out in the desert and I got there about a week before the 82d did.

So, I was out in this big camp with all these tents waiting on the 82d to show up and there's maybe like twenty people setting up the camp. So, I stayed there about a week and finally the 82d showed up. So, when the 82d got there, we immediately started planning to jump into Baghdad. When George Bush gave the go ahead, we were going to jump into Baghdad and take down the airport and do what the 82d does, and set up an airfield there. So, we trained and trained, we had models of the airport, we studied the maps, we studied all the models, I think they spent something like twenty thousand dollars on that model; it was huge. It was probably like a twenty by twenty model, you know like a sandbox. And we studied that thing every day, planning that airborne operation into Baghdad, and we were just waiting on George Bush to give the go ahead. And we also went out to Failaka Island, off the coast of Kuwait, and did a bunch of training out there in a building that was very similar to all the buildings in Iraq. We did a lot of training there, for little things, like making sure our rucksacks would fit through the hallways, you know, because their hallways are small and narrow. So, we did a lot training out on that island and also come back and study the airport.

At some point, I guess someone decided that if we tried to jump into the airport, that we'd never make it, we'd never hit the ground. Someone decided that they'd shoot the airplanes out of the sky before we even got over the airport. So, that decision was made, probably a couple of days before George Bush gave the go ahead to go into Iraq. We didn't know exactly where we were going to cross the border. We just kept waiting, everyday training, studying maps, that kinda stuff. And then one day the order was given that we would get ammo. So, we all lined up, the whole camp, it was a Brigade of 82d guys. So, we all lined up, we got ammo, we got hand grenades, we got AT-4s for shooting tanks, all that kinda stuff. So, we knew that this was gonna happen, cause now we all got ammo and hand grenades. One of the first told me to get an AT-4, and I told him no, I'm not carrying an AT-4, and he says oh yes you are, all the NCOs are carrying AT-4s. And I told him all the NCOs aren't carrying radios and batteries like I do, so I'm not carrying an AT-4. So, anyway, the next day after we got our ammo, we got in our Humvees and we drove up to the border of Kuwait and Iraq. The 3rd ID and the Marines were already racing to Baghdad with their tanks and basically they were fighting their way to Baghdad and leaving a big army behind them. And so the 82d's mission was to go in and clean up this big army that they were leaving behind them. We drove the first day into an airfield in southern Iraq and we spent the night there.

Then the next day we drove into a town, Asamawah. The town of Asamawah had a battalion of uniformed Iraqis that we were supposed to go kick butt and run them out of town. What they told us the whole time was that every time we made contact with the army they would capitulate. They would basically lay their weapons down and surrender. They did that during the first Gulf War, so what they kept telling us, was when you guys make contact with these Iraqis, they're just gonna surrender, there's not going to be a fight. We went into the town of Asamawah, and remember, I'd been in Afghanistan for eight months, well in Afghanistan, like I told you, we kinda ruled the country. We'd go in, we'd make contact, they'd fire a few shots, then run away since we had so much firepower. Well, that's kinda what I thought was going to happen in Iraq. I found out real quick that two things didn't happen; they didn't capitulate and we didn't just rule the place like we did in Afghanistan. This battalion of uniformed Iraqis in Asamawah, they were dug in and they were strong and they were ready to fight. And that's exactly what they did.

The first day we were there I was moving with an 82d Airborne company and it was me and my teammate. We were the only two Air Force guys in the unit; we were their forward air controllers. We were with them; we were walking right down the road. Now you know, always in training, you always train not to walk in the road; you're just an open target. But, that's what we did when we moved into Asamawah, walked right down the road and it turns out we walked right into, they saw us coming from miles away – you know the desert's flat, so they saw us coming – they were waiting on us. They were dug in on both sides of the road to our left and to our right. They had set up a mortar firing position about a kilometer away, from where they were dug in. The mortar firing position was off to our East and it was about a kilometer. So we walked right into this

ambush. Like I said, they were dug in on both
sides of the road, so we caught right in the
middle. They were dug into our front, they were
dug into our rear – we had walked right passed
them and didn't see them. They were real well
camouflaged, and used a lot of great
concealment techniques. So, when we walked
right into where they wanted us, the fire started
coming from our rear, it was coming from our
front and we started taking mortar fire from that
mortar position about a kilometer to our East. It
was very effective fire. I'd been in firefights in
Afghanistan, small skirmishes, and thought I got
a little taste of the fog of war. But, I had no idea
of what the fog of war was until this day.
Because, when the fire started it was so
confusing, no one knew who was shooting, we
didn't know if the Iraqis were shooting at us, or
if we were shooting at them. It was hard to tell
where the fire was coming from, except the
bullets were hitting right in front of us, so, we
knew the Iraqis were shooting at us, but we
didn't know where it was coming from. It turns
out, in hindsight, it was coming from our front
and our rear. And then these mortars were
coming down right on top of us. Within, I'd say
forty five seconds of this ambush right out of the
corner of my eye I see a streak coming and it
was an RPG. I thought it was coming right for
me. I was within five feet, we had one Humvee
with us, it had a .50 caliber machine gun
mounted on top of it. We were all on foot and
we had one Humvee and had the .50 caliber
machine gun that was returning fire. The RPG
hit that Humvee, our gun truck. I was within
five feet of the truck. When the RPG hit the

truck, I took the blast when the thing exploded, because I was within five feet of it on the same side as it hit. The blast threw me off the road into the ditch. Now, of course I was stunned from the explosion, I was checking myself to see if I'd been hit. I thought I had been hit. The concussion, I thought I was messed up, but of course I wasn't. I had been on the radio and of course there's gunfire in the background during the ambush, so on the radio on the other end is Mike C. He was at the aviation brigade, so he can hear me yelling calling for air, the gunfire and all that. That's when the RPG hit and of course my teammate went one we and I went the other and of course the radio went silent. So, Mike C. thought I was dead. He was at the aviation brigade at the TOC and they said that he had the hand mic to his ear, then when he heard the explosion and then the radio went silent, he threw the hand mic in the TOC and yelled out, 'No!' cause he thought I was dead, until we came back up on the radio. Now I'm trying to find my teammate, he was my radio guy. He had the radios we used to call for an airstrike, and I had the radio we used to talk to the aircraft. So, I needed his radio and he needed me. We were separated now, and I didn't know if he was alive or dead, I couldn't find him. I couldn't yell for him because it was so loud with all the gunfire. I looked up and the Humvee was on fire, flames were coming out the windows, but the gunner, till the day I die, I'll see that gunner, flames were coming out the turret and that gunner was still returning fire. Like his truck is on fire and that guys still hammering down on the .50 caliber, returning fire.

Now, I'm crawling back onto the road, I'm afraid of being shot at this point, bullets were hitting everywhere, the dust was flying from the bullets hitting everywhere. But, I had to find my teammate, because he's got the radio – we need airpower – and my teammate's got the radio. I crawl back on the road to find him. His name's Rudy, he was nineteen years old. I crawl back up on the road to find him and lo and behold he's on the other side of the road in the ditch. My first thought was, I hope he's alive. So, as I'm going toward him, he's coming toward me, so I know he's alive. So, I yell at him, 'Rudy, you gotta call the battalion and send us some airplanes.' We had airplanes over Asamawah, because we were doing push CAS – which means, the airplane is already there waiting for someone who needs them. I knew the airplanes were overhead, so I told Rudy, 'You gotta call battalion and tell them to get come airplanes over here,' because that's the only thing that's going to take care of this. So, Rudy's calling battalion and asking for the airpower. I start trying to find the ground commander; he's a Captain, because he's the company commander. I'm trying to find him to let him know I've got air coming and that the first thing I'm going to do is drop on this mortar position and I need his approval and I need to know what his plans are to drop on this mortar position because the 82d is returning fire, but this mortar position, you can't return fire on that, we need airpower to take that thing out. So, I'm looking for the ground commander, and I can't find him. I found his radio guy and said, 'Where's the ground commander?' And his radio guy says, 'He ran.' What I thought he meant was that he ran for cover, and that he's trying to collect himself and try to figure out what we're going to do to get out of this bad situation. But, it turns out he ran, like a coward, he ran away. And so, I thought now, the ground commander's gone, there's a platoon in front of us, that's fighting the fire that's coming from our front, and a platoon, I hope, that's fighting the fire that's coming from behind us. Well, it turns out the platoon that was in the rear when the ground commander ran they saw him run, and like they should, they followed their commander. So, the trail platoon, they ran with their commander. So, now we have no rear, however, they are returning fire as they're retreating. The lead platoon, at some point figures out that they have no rear; that the trail platoon had run. Now I look up and here comes the lead platoon, they're coming right at me. Rudy's calling the battalion for air and they sent us some. There was another JTAC, Dusty, with another company that was closer to that mortar position than me. I knew where they were on the map – being a good JTAC I knew where all the friendlies were. I knew where he was, and he was calling battalion at the same time to tell them, 'Hey look, I see that mortar firing position that's firing at Alpha company,' which was the company that I was with. So, as we are trying to get out of this kill zone, and trying to find the ground commander, the whole thing went right down the pipes as the trail platoon ran away, and now the lead platoon's trying to get out of there, because they've got no rear. I am now talking to this other JTAC to see if I can get the aircraft over to him so he can take out this mortar position that's still firing at us.

In the meantime, the Humvee that's on fire is in reverse, the tires are melted and this thing is rolling backwards and trying to get out of the kill sack, is what we called it. Anyway, as I'm talking to this other JTAC he knows exactly where this mortar position is, so I tell him I've got two A-10s and I'm going to pass them over to him and take out that mortar position. Well, I try to pass the A-10s over to him, and I found out that during the explosion, when it knocked me off the road and onto the ground, I must have landed on my antenna, because my antenna on the radio is broke. I can't get the airplane because my antenna on my radio is broken. Of course, I didn't know this until they kept calling me and I kept calling them and we couldn't communicate. I finally took my radio off my back, and I look and the antenna is laid over and wires are hanging out of it. So, our radio maintenance guys had made these little field expedient emergency antennas, so I pulled my antenna off, right in the middle of this firefight and stuck this field expedient antenna on. So, now I'm communicating with the A-10s. I told the A-10s, I gave them a quick update to where the mortar firing position was. So, when they went to the other JTAC, they knew where we were, because I gave them friendly locations, told them that we were pulling back about a kilometer from where we were, at this point, moving south down the road. I passed them off to the other JTAC and talked them on to the mortar firing position, so they knew where it was. And basically, I passed them off to him and he did confirmatory communication with them to make sure we were talking about the same firing position and he gave them the cleared hot call to drop on those mortars, and he did.

At some point, the enemy had brought children out around those mortar tubes to use as human shields, because the Iraqis were hoping that the Americans wouldn't drop on children. I called the battalion and told them, 'Hey, they've got children out around these mortar tubes,' and battalion made a quick call to brigade, and the brigade commander said there was nothing he could do, you gotta take out those mortar tubes, it doesn't matter who's around them. So, it's just something you kinda have to live with, innocent people died, they didn't die by our hands, although we dropped the bombs on them, it was the Iraqis who got them killed that day. We took out those mortars and the 82d was able to pull back and regroup without those mortars killing us. The 82d real good at returning fire, but you can't fight mortars. The only thing you can do is either stop them, or get out of the way. We were able to drop some 500lbs bombs on those mortars and took 'em out. Once those 500lb'ers dropped the shooting stopped, the mortars stopped, I think the Iraqis took a big morale blow, because all the small arms stopped and they all ran away. Once those 500lb'ers dropped on those mortars, they knew they had no more support after that. We pulled back about a kilometer; we regrouped. We went back up to our objective, we were trying to take a bridge on the Euphrates River; that was the whole point, that's where we were moving to in

the first place. We went back up to that bridge
after a couple hours of planning. We did some
preparatory fires, basically we shot artillery all
up that road before we made any movement.
We took our objective a few hours later. Up on
that objective, we took more resistance. There
was actually a military barracks up there. They
were shooting right down that same road at us.
Rudy and I, my teammate, all along that road
there was fire coming straight down the road at
us. We laid on our bellies, by this point it was
night time, we laid on our bellies and hit the, lit
the target up with our IZLID, our pointer, and
we took out that barracks. After we took out
that barracks we used F-14s, for that, it was
actually a female pilot, had two F-14s from the
Navy show up and we dropped a 1000lb'er on
the building first. And then the fire stopped.
When that 1000lb'er hit that barracks, it dud'ed
out, it didn't explode, but at least the fire
stopped. Once we figured out it was a dud, I
was first afraid she didn't hit the target, but turns
out it was a dud, we got her back around and she
dropped another 1000lb'er on it and the building
exploded. There was a combat controller on the
other side of that building watching that thing
and he said that when that dud went into that
barracks, people ran out of the thing and he
watched, and by the time she came back around
and we got her back on the target, they were
going back in the building to see this big hole
this dud had made, then we got the 1000lb'er in
on it and the building exploded. The guys that
had run away, they came back and we got them
anyway. Anyway, that was my first day, I guess
my second day, since we spent one night, so my

second day in Iraq and the Battle of Asamawah. The whole war went just about like that. They weren't there to capitulate; they were dug in just like that. After we figured that out, the gloves came off and we did well after that. Well, that's my story." Josh and I chatted for a little bit longer and he added;

"You know, I never talked to that company commander much after that. With all the drops in further engagements, I never really talked to him. We had a really strong first sergeant; he was a good infantryman. The first sergeant and I kinda ran the company after that, to be honest with you, because we weren't gonna let anybody else die."

Josh retired after a great career of leadership and operational accomplishments. Josh was always most concerned about taking care of the Airmen. When it came to the situation, Josh always gave it to you straight. In my entire career I'd have to say, he was the guy I trusted the most. Josh undoubtedly saved many, many lives, directly in combat, but also in how he trained his subordinates to do the dangerous and unforgiving job of Tactical Air Control. He retired and opened up a nursery in his home state and is enjoying his lovely wife and two growing boys.

Baghdad International Airport - "Secured"

****

Vet: *"Shrop"*
Setting: *The Ale House outside of Fort Hood, Texas. Shrop and I were both there on the job working the latest Warfighter Exercise.*
Drinks: *Shrop had a Guinness Blonde and I had a real beer, a Guinness Pub Draught.*

Story: "You want me to talk really loud, you want ME TO TALK LIKE THIS?"

I said, "No, just talk normal, wiseguy."

"So, we're at the 20th ASOS and I got sent to PSAB at the CAOC for a while, I think that's where I ran into you. One, you asked if I had the SOF train up. I didn't have that two-week bullshit that you guys required, but whatever. And then you asked me, 101st or 3rd Infantry Division, and I said, 3rd Infantry Division. Because I'd already seen some of the planning at the CAOC. So, I knew who was going to go up there and who was going to guarding supplies – Sorry, 19th and 14th! So, then Voight looks at me and says, 'Careful what you wish for Shropshire.' I said, 'Ok, I know what I'm getting myself into.' But I had no idea.

I was working in the SOLE so I was hopping rides over to Ali Al Salem with some of the SF guys. I get into this place and it's twelve dudes looking at a map and they say, 'Dude, this is where you're going.' I was like, no, no I'm going with Colonel Risner, with the 15th ASOS, that's what I'm ordered to do. And they said, 'No, you're going to be with us.' I couldn't break away from those guys forever. Eventually I was able to find the TACPs, or they found me. And they said, 'Hey, Colonel Risners on the phone and he's pissed off.' So, I picked up the SAT phone and he's like, 'Where the fuck are you!?' He's really mad. I didn't even get a chance to explain it to him and he said he was going to send some people out to get me. Now when I was at COAC up at PSAB, the food was awesome; Mongolian bar-b-que, chocolate chip cookies, and Air Force wet dream, with food. I get out there, we're driving up near Camp New York, there's this huge pillar of black smoke – the chow hall was burning down. So, we went immediately to MREs and T-rats in the evenings. I was like God dang it.

They put me with 3rd of 7th Cavalry under Colonel Farrell. I was with Crazy Horse Troop, C-Troop with Captain McCoy. They were great. We had to move out of the tents and move out into the desert so they 101st and those guys could take the tents. I really started bonding with these guys; it was really awesome. Some if the guys brought out the little DVD players and jerry-rigged them so they could watch movies and stuff and they were watching We Were Soldiers, the 7th Cav guys out there with Hal Moore in Vietnam and we were joking about that, 'Oh yeah, we're 7th Cav, what are we gonna get surrounded and cut off…eww…' I'm paraphrasing the snobbery, but… Should have seen that one coming; that was a black cat crossing our path. Not that there's anything wrong with black cats.

So, flash forward, we're moving through the desert. These guys really learned their lesson from Desert Storm. They did not sit out in the open desert like they did twelve years prior. They pulled their asses back and they were going to fight us more in an urban setting. So, the very first engagement, I had lost my track right when we crossed the border. That stupid piece of junk broke down. And not like when the Millennium Falcon freakin breaks down, wee, woo, woo, woo, woo. I'm running around grabbing bags and stuff, and they're like, 'Catch up!' I get passed from Brad to Brad then they put me in a mortar track. That's what I was in when we got to the first city. We get up there and we secure the canal bridges and we start getting shot at. What do we do when we first get shot at? We don't shoot back. We stand around looking at each other, 'Are they shooting at us?' One thing led to another and finally we backed up we fought that fight and I even hung some mortar rounds on that one. We came out ok and instead of finishing off the city; we went around it, 'cause we had to do our job as the Cav.

Eventually we got ourselves near An Najaf, actually An Najaf was north of us, we were in Abu Sukura, if that's how you pronounce it, something like that. We were to stay on those bridges, a Cav squadron was moving to the north and our troop was to keep that bridge, because tanks are heavy, not a lot of bridges over there, especially across the Euphrates. So, that's what we did. Everybody talks about the sand storm hitting, like it was out of the movie, The Mummy or something, I don't remember it that way. I just remember it being really sandy. Maybe I wasn't paying attention to the sky or something like that. I almost felt like it happened instantly. It just sucked. It was complete garbage; you can't see, you can't breath. We crossed the bridge and almost instantly, the little bastards popped up from underneath the bridge. They were popping out from little spider holes. They were right with us, right there. The armor guys didn't want to bury themselves in their tanks, they were hanging out of the tanks, they were fighting with small arms. You can't fight dismounts with a tank at close range. You've got to fight 'em with your hands. The tanks turn into pillboxes almost, with pudding on the top, with a nugget center called a US soldier. There they are, I can't see anything and I keep thinking the whole time, what are we going to do? We've got to do airstrikes. I didn't figure we'd have to do anything because if we couldn't see, they couldn't see. I was wrong, dead wrong, or they were dead wrong.

As it progressed, I'm skipping around here, but I'm trying to highlight the important parts I guess. I'm on the radio and I'm talking, and I don't feel like I know what I'm saying half the time, at least I don't remember. I was trying to relay the information as best as I see it. Which is less than ten or fifteen feet and I think we're getting surrounded. I'm paraphrasing, but I think I told somebody on the radio that we were getting surrounded. It kinda just rolled from there. There were just more and more and more of them. They just kept pouring into the area. They were pouring trucks in there. They were pouring in dismounted infantry. It looked like they were all working together, those Fedayeen cheese heads, the Iraqi police, guys dressed as civilians, I'm sure there was a spattering of regular military here and there. It was really weird. Later on I found out we were what the military loves to call their 'bait,' which is a 'feint.' Thanks. I guess it makes sense.

They were pouring into the area and were just fighting, just fighting. But we were fighting, it was like the tanks and the tracks turned into individual fortresses. They were zipping in between us, all kinds of stuff. It is a miracle that none of our guys got hit. The volume of fire was so high, it was snapping off the antennas. It was crazy. They were running trucks down with guys in the back. You ever see those movies from like India were they've got every swinging Joe on the back of those trucks like it was gonna tip. That's the way those trucks looked like, bringing them down into the mix. They were even taking some field trucks and were ramming them into the tanks, which, spectacular explosion by the way. Just nothing like the movies, it doesn't last that long. Except for the smoke and the horrible explosion. Anyway, this guy gets off one of the vehicles and the Bradleys just beat this truck up, one of the few times they were able to use their COAX. A guy gets close to our track and let's loose with an AK and hits the SATCOM antenna. It was weird it really didn't hurt the antenna, but snapped a few of the wires, didn't hurt it too bad. I got some tape and taped it together, you know you're equipment. We had HF as a backup, which was ready to go. It was a little nerve racking, but it still worked. That guy; died, because, he missed me and I got him. I didn't drawn down on him, I didn't do any kinda Rambo shit to him, all I did was, as the bullets were passing me, I started pulling the trigger on what I had and I got lucky and he didn't. There was no skill involved. Just the way it happened. I'll take that. There were a few more guys. We were going back and forth, and the gist of it is, we fought them off enough to where we got the airstrikes on and at some point the guys were protecting my track with soldiers. We were running black on ammo for small arms. We were picking AKs and whatever we could get off the bodies, PKMs, all that stuff.

At one point it started raining. So, I was like, 'Seriously God, I mean come on.' But, the aircraft stayed on and they did a great job. We had them stacked up and they just beat the shit out of that area. Then it got really quiet. I don't know if you remember this or not, somebody called up and said that the JSTARS had spotted tanks moving in, or what they thought was armor. Well, you remember all the false hits we were getting, on camels and stuff like that. I didn't know if that was true or not, and I would never do this again, but I did it here and somebody wrote it in the citation, and I need to kick them in the butt, because when I read that, I mean when my wife heard that she said, 'Really? You're a dumbass.'

The only long-haul communications we had was the SATCOM antenna and they cleared the net so that Captain McCoy could talk to Colonel Farrell. Apparently, he gave this awesome speech that everyone heard. I never heard it. I don't even know what he said. I only heard McCoy's part, which was mainly, 'Uh, we're screwed.' I guess Colonel Farrell gave him some great speech that motivated him and then we were on target. So, anyway, there's still a lot of sand in the air and there's a freakin tank, right in front of us. Not our tank! It was a bad tank, an Iraqi tank, which is a lot bigger when you're close to it. So, I get back up there, I'm breathing heavy (Shrop had gotten out of his track and ran forward to verify what the JSTARS, an Air Force reconnaissance plane that picked up moving targets, was telling them about an incoming tank formation.) Somebody had actually asked if they were trying to capitulate, which was a load of crap. They weren't. So, they got me a B-1. I decided to use the B-1 in such a way that a lot of the guys I learned from who were in Desert Storm and a lot of the guys who fought some of the battles, even though it was only a hundred hours, there were several battles during that time. If they were overwhelmed with firepower, a lot of them backed up. Not to mention how the Russian armor was built, which is what they were using, why the turrets pop off they way they do, and all of that stuff. I didn't factor this in out of sheer genius, I factored it in due to sheer training and listening to those guys who put so much time, the guys in the Cold War era who spent so much time researching and looking into how to defeat all these systems and all this armor and stuff like that. Those were my bosses. I just took a little slice of the Fulda Gap and threw it into this. So, the B-1 shows up and he's got twelve GBU-31 JDAMs and I used two of them right off the git go, boom, and right behind them. I taught the soldiers before we crossed into Iraq not to give me some complicated talk on, if you can see something just give me, from last bomb, a cardinal direction and distance. That's what this guy did. There was one private who was like, 'Holy shit man, they're still here shooting at me.' I was like, 'Where are they?' He said, 'Five Hundred meters west.' So, I called it up to the B-1 to drop two again. I called it the hammer and anvil. You can do that with anything, but I did it with two bombs at a time. Hammer and anvil; had the anvil right here, right in front of them then the hammer right in back of them. And it worked. I don't know why, it just worked. It had broken up the attack. I don't know exactly how many of them there were, but it looked like a butt-load afterwards as we looked over there, as we were moving. I guess it worked out for us.

That next morning, there were so many dudes just lying around dead. We didn't take one casualty. That's...I don't know how many times that's happened in history, in American fighting forces, but thank God. Somebody stupidly once told me that '...if we'd lost a couple of soldiers I would have gotten a better medal...' I said that I would have taken a bar of chocolate for not losing one soldier. That's a good day. That's a great day. Screw the medal – and I like chocolate. You'd think they'd bury their dead, but there was nobody around. There was a lot of gruesome stuff, what the bombs did and all the other stuff. There's this dude walking and he's got his man-dress on and he's got black boots and green pants underneath. Wait a sec... I jump down and I get the interpreter over. He's Republican Guard but he's stripped a lot of his stuff off of his uniform. Why he was walking by us I don't know. They let him go. We were so spent. One dude was no threat. I've left some things out, but that was the gist of what happened.

I get both sides of it. I got a lot of haters and I got a lot of pats on the back. I really didn't know what to do with it. I didn't know where to go with it. All I knew for sure was that I was more comfortable over there, then going home and I wanted to keep fighting. Like I said, I didn't know what to do with it, I didn't know how, I don't know, funnel it, or channel it, but I had a lot of great leadership and mentorship that helped me funnel and channel it. One of the things I did was volunteer to go to NTC, which was unheard of to volunteer to go to NTC. I got lucky; I got a great crew of dudes and we came up with a concept they called the CAS sticks line. It was series of situational training. It was one problem after another and just take them out of the COIN mentality and back into a combat mentality at a company level and brigade and battalion. They loved it. It was an overwhelming success. We didn't own the lane, the community owned the lane, so we improved it every time. When dudes would see me or interact with me, they'd go, 'Oh, you're that guy, blah, blah, blah...' I would say, 'Let me tell you where I screwed up and where I was successful. Now, let's go out here and do this, and apply some of that.' We would get emails that would say, 'I thought your scenario was bullshit, but it just happened to me...' We were real happy about that. When you train guys hard, make sure they know their equipment; it's a big thing. They know their job. It doesn't matter where they are, they're applying those skill sets necessary and the end result is no matter how many dudes they bomb or equipment they blow up, whatever, it all comes down to saving soldiers. That's all that matters. That didn't happen overnight for me. That took a long time to put into perspective over time. Like we talked about earlier, war does weird things to you. There was one time a guy comes out with an AK-47 and starts shooting it in the air. Everybody hits the deck and they want me to get air in on that one guy, that wasn't shooting at us. You train your dudes and you take all that stuff... I don't know where I'm going with all this, but there are guys who get medals and they waste it. They got the medal, that moment was great, but then they don't do anything with it. Now you have more of a duty and responsibility to help your fellow service members out. A medal is not, 'hey you're awesome', it's in this event, with these sets of circumstances you set a standard, and this is what you got. Everybody who looks at that... exceed that standard, if you find yourself in a similar situation. That's how I look at it. It's a kind of street cred I guess to help train these guys. It's been a pain in the ass too, getting that medal, standing up there, I'm not a very articulate guy. Sometimes, I'm a dude that likes to go out and fight. I like my radios and I like my job and I like this community. That's about it."

Shrop was awarded the Silver Star for his actions during Operation Iraqi Freedom. He served in various positions of increasing responsibility and requested a posting at the National Training Center, for the purpose of helping those that follow him be better prepared for combat. Shrop chalked up his success to his ability to listen and take to heart the teachings and advice of the grey beards, the silver back gorillas of the squadron and put those lessons to practical use in a high intensity combat situation. Shrop spent a few years out there in the California desert doing just that. No telling how many lives he saved by passing on his lessons learned to the young troops that followed. He recently retired, but took a job in which he continues to advise and assist his brothers and sisters still serving.

****

Vet: "Joe H."
Setting: Joe's House
Drinks: Imperial Stout

Story: "It was my first trip to Iraq. I had combat experience from Operation Anaconda, so they put me on the QRF. I sat in the QRF building for like three months. We were sending the other guys up to Sadr City to get experience and they were doing AC-130 missions like crazy. They were seriously wrecking stuff up there. So, we start hearing about the build up in Fallujah. They said that they were definitely going to send bodies in there, we were going to go door to door and clear this place back out, we were taking it back. So, I get called into the Division Headquarters and they were like, 'Hey, we've got a mission for you.' I'm like, 'Ok, cool.' They said, 'What we're going to do is go out to camp Fallujah, we're going to sit out there for a while, do some recon in the area and then we're going to start from the north and work our way south and we're going to take that whole AO.' I asked, 'Where do I come into play on this?' They took me and Chris M. and we went in with a Special Ops Team in the back of a Bradley. We spent a couple of days doing recon in the area.

The (enemy) snipers were really awesome in Fallujah. I give them a lot of props, we couldn't locate them and they were notorious for screwing with us. They'd wiz a bullet by our heads just to be like, surprise son-of-a-bitch...we can shack you right now if we wanted to. We kept going up there in Bradleys and I can't remember if it was a Special Ops guy or a

Marine and they were shooting them right in the body armor just to prove a point, shattering the body armor. That had us nervous. So, it changed our tactic of going in at night instead of the daytime. The General at the time, the Marines handle things differently in their AO, which is awesome, he comes out and briefs all of us, JTACs and SOF guys, '...if it moves, kill it. I don't care who it is, what it is, they've had time to get out of there. At this point just kill it. If you see a muzzle flash from a building, shoot a tank round through it. Just go in there and annihilate the place...You guys kick ass and take back that city and we'll all have a beer after this.'

The night of the attack, we had a battalion of 1st Cav Division that was going to take the northeastern side of the city. Like I said, I was going in with the Special Ops guys until they took the objective and then ideally, I'd get sliced off and go work with one of the CAV battalions, or something like that, or at least one of the companies. So, we set up and spend one night where the battalion TOC is set up. The next day we start prepping for everything. We had me, Chris M., two Special Ops guys in our Bradley, some Fire Support weenie that took up like three quarters of the other side of it. I mean he was good to go. We got the briefing that what the Marines were gonna do was stand shoulder to shoulder, all the way down the north berm of this entire city, the Sergeant Major is going to blow a whistle, they're going to have fixed bayonets and they're going to charge the city. We thought that was pretty funny, that they were making fun of the Marines.

That night prep fires were insane. It was awesome; it was like ten hours of buildings blowing up, artillery, airstrikes, all these prep fires that were going on. It looked like the Fourth of July. Me and a couple of the Special Ops guys were sitting on the Bradleys; it was like awesome. It was like the Fourth of July, but it was straight up death and destruction. It's getting to be about an hour out until we're ready to assault the city. Still stuff blowing up and flashes out there. Then they start to move closer to us. Then we see bodies standing up on the berm. Maybe they're just trying to draw attention. My ROMAD grabs some NVGs and he's like, 'I'll be damned, they really doing it.' He hands me the NVGs and sure enough there are Marines, as far as the eye can see, all the way down. They were going to do what they said they were going to do. Time comes for the assault, the Sergeant Majors all blow their whistles and the Marines all take off like a bat out of hell into town. We're like, holy shit this is actually happening. By the time they get to the edge of the city and start going door to door, the engineers are going to blow the berm and all the Bradleys are going to go through. This is all happening on the north side of the city too. We hop on in, we secure the hatch and we start hearing the Bangalores blowing up all the damn berms and we go in.

We sat in the back of that damn Bradley for thirteen, no, it was seventeen hours. It was hot, cramped. We were trying to assault our main objective, the school. We were going to make that our command post and headquarters and start moving out from there. Seventeen hours we sat there, and I stared at this fat kid eating his MREs and looking at the backdoor. That's really a weak spot of the Bradley; shoot an RPG and your done. We were constantly staring at that back hatch wondering when it was going to happen, when's it going to happen? The gunner up on top was getting in some good action. You could hear the 240, or the chain gun and he was taking dudes out, it was pretty cool.

We finally get to the objective. It's the next day and it's dark. There's probably a platoon of Joes right on the south side of it. And they're just throwing hand grenades like crazy, that's how they're clearing everything, just throwing hand grenades through windows, everywhere. I'm like, what the hell? We get out, me and the two Special Ops guys are going to link up with another two SOF guys from the other vehicle and move to another objective. Me and my ROMAD, we're going to clear this school. This is probably the dumbest thing I've thought of; there are not a lot of us. We put on our kit, put on our NVGs, we got our goggles on and we drop the ramp. We move out and we're entirely cramped and dehydrated. We can't do squat. We're tripping over shit; we're lying on the ground all cramped up. We hadn't moved in seventeen hours. We go be-bopping into the place, my goggles are so fogged up, but my NVGs still worked. The helmet mount for my NVGs broke so I had to carry them on my face. Now this is great. Now I'm clearing a room with a 9 mil because that's the only way I can work it. We're going top to bottom on that thing. Adrenalin is flowing, not a damn thing was in that place. We found a teacher that the

Iraqis had shot. They shot her in the head, and then they shot her in the uterus and all that area down there. Apparently, from what our terp [Interpreter] was saying, they didn't want us to have sex with their women. So, they just executed a woman like that. We finally get settled in and start pulling a watch shift so guys can get racked out. That was it for the night.

I wake up from my shift and it was actually daytime already. Rockets are just ripping up and down the streets. The Iraqis are just screwing us pretty hard. They sucked at shooting, but they're just having a hay day. There's a gigantic-assed building on the north part of one of the main routes, eight to ten stories and right in front of it was that main road that went out of the city. That's where they dragged those guys and burned them and hung them from the bridge. It was maybe a block in from right there. So, from that day, we were taking a lot of sniper fire from that building. The stuff we did with the SOF guys was pretty uneventful. I had more fun with the Army units we supported a couple of days into it. We started shooting Javelins into the buildings. It's pretty sweet shooting a Javelin in the first place, it goes way up and comes straight down and just schwacks the hell out of the building. So, we shoot a bunch of Javelins and once again we're taking fire. I'm having a really tough time getting anyone up on Fox Mike on the comms. So, anyways, we have a fire mission going on to take out one of the buildings in front of it and then we're going to figure out what to do with the main building. All of a sudden the rounds start hitting right across the street. We've got four Bradleys parked down the street and we're watching these rounds walk their way in on top of the Bradleys. They hit right where we were trying to have them hit, then instead of walking them out, they were walking them in. One actually did actually hit the first Bradley. It didn't do much to it, with the reactive armor. It actually didn't wreck the Bradley; I was pretty impressed. We call up and tell them to knock it off. More rockets start coming up the street aimed at the Bradleys, but they're missing left and right and hitting houses all along the street.

The SOF guys were doing their thing; the snipers were shooting all night, also shooting out the speakers on one of the mosques. It was annoying the hell out of us. I come up and I say, 'What have we got going on?' They say, 'Well, we're going to take that building down over there.' That's the one we're having all the issues with. I asked if I was going with them, they said no, they were going to keep it just amongst them. I was looking at the JTAC SOF guy with me, Adam, and asked if he was going, and he said no. It was a dumb idea. Long story short, they ended up trying to take down the building and all of them ended up getting air-evac'ed back to Germany and stateside, 'cause they got fucked up.

I was calling in missions periodically. We created keyhole CAS during that operation; that was kind of a new thing. I was more focused on shooting back at dudes. I had a grenade launcher so I was lobbing rounds into windows. I was pretty sure I got a few guys who were shooting out the windows. We had periodic firefights; nothing overly insane. The next day we go further into town and capture more objectives. We take this building down, one of the snipers that was with us, he was schwacking guys left and right, he goes in to take down this building. He went in first and caught some resistance at the door. They throw in a hand grenade and it frags the guy, kills him deader than shit. They go in quietly and they hear this voice, calling out for that guy, kinda like, 'Hey Bob, you there Bob, Bob, Bob...' The guy was hiding in like a closet area in back of the kitchen. So they take a grenade and lob it in there, and take him out. So, we drag the two bodies out and establish the building for the day.

The first night, we're sitting up on the roof setting up an observation point. We kept getting fire from the east side. We were constantly getting in firefights from that direction. We'd go up on the wall, shooting down the alleys, shooting down the streets. We probably blew about 10,000 rounds when we were up on that roof. The ROMAD's like, 'I gotta go take a shit.' We're up on the very top floor, and you go down a flight of stairs and that next floor down was where the bathroom was. We're sitting there and sure enough they start screwing with us again. All of a sudden we hear this explosion on the side of the house. One of the guys looks over and he says, 'Damn it!' and we start shooting at a building on the opposite corner. Eventually we send over a Bradley and smoke the shooters. The ROMAD hurries up doing what he was doing and comes back up stairs and sits down. He's sitting there, starts calming down, then says, 'Look what landed in my lap.' It was the spoon of a grenade. I was like, 'Dude, you realize, he was trying to throw that grenade at you in the shitter.' He couldn't get it all the way to the roof so it bounced off the ceiling of the floor he was on. My ROMAD would have been fragged while sitting on the shitter. I was thinking, how do I write home to his parents, 'Hey your son died honorably taking a crap in the middle of a firefight.'

So, that night we get some gunships on station and did some small missions, called for some prep fires for building clearing teams, basically shooting some 105s into buildings in support of the clearing ops. Basically, Marines were getting hit pretty damn hard. We were watching some Marines clearing a building, they were moving from one to the next and as soon as they came around the wall surrounding the building three of them were mowed down. There was a heavy machinegun sitting right in that house. The fourth was approaching the kill zone and were like, 'Get back, don't go,' and he went around the corner and he got wacked too. The guy took out four dudes. So, they asked me, can I hit that machinegun position, and I was like, 'Yeah.' I called in a gunship and hit a couple other positions like that.

Another weird story, we're looking over in one direction and saw that some of our tanks were starting to come through. We're getting down into the southern area and they're really starting to get resistance. The tanks were advancing down south. Every other street we'd have Bradleys set up for security, one looking one direction and on the next street they'd be looking the other way. We hear some chatter on the radio and look in the direction of one of the

Bradleys. A guy starts running toward them and all of a sudden, just after the Bradley starts opening up, we hear a poof and look up and it's maybe four or five stories in the air we see the torso of a guy flying through the air. He must have had a suicide vest on and they turned the chain gun on him and it detonated. Blew this dude like a hundred feet into the air. It was entertaining for us; anything is entertaining in combat. That night snipers pinned us down all night. We controlled more gunships, didn't do much with fighters at the time. We try to get some sleep and in the middle of the night, everything is getting lit up. I woke up, 'What the hell?' I look over and I see tracer rounds coming over our roof. One of the guys was like, 'Get down, shit's going down.' I look down and my ROMAD is still out, sound asleep. The enemy rounds start zeroing in on us, hitting the wall above us, so I get down and roll over top of my ROMAD, with my flak vest, my body armor and I pull it over him. He wakes up and he's like, 'Get off me fag, I don't play that way.' And I yelled, 'Stay still.' One of the rounds hit my body armor then bounced off the wall and the chunk of metal hit the floor next to us. We both looked at it, 'Damn.' Now every year my ROMAD reminds me that I saved his life. Actually, had I not done that that round would have caught him in his sleep and killed him. This kid was death prone, I swear to God. He almost gets killed on the shitter and he almost took a round in his sleep. He was determined not to go out with an honorable death, if it was going to happen in Fallujah.

We started to get further south. These
guys started hiding out in Mosques, the General
was like, 'We don't care, we're taking out
Mosques.' Now the jets are going out and we're
dropping Mosques throughout the city. Once we
started doing that, it was like we stirred up a
hornet's nest. They had thought they'd found a
safe haven hiding and shooting at us from the
Mosques, now that we were fighting back
everything ratcheted up a notch. This is now
four or five days into it. Most of the other
JTACs and ROMADs from my squadron were
already back home. We were still out there, me
and Chris M. We ended up sitting in this
building for a day and shooting pigeons. It was
kinda funny. You know how they all line up.
You take one out, the others wouldn't fly off, the
next one in line would just shuffle over to where
the one that just got shot was and all of them
would slide down a position. You'd shoot one,
they'd all crowd together, 'Oops, there goes
Bob.' The dogs were starting to become an
issue down in the southern area because of all
the dead bodies. This was almost week into the
fight. We had a standing order to shoot dogs,
which kinda sucked. We had the same thing in
Afghanistan around Bagram. There was a dead
body right in the middle of the street near the
big-assed house we had. Nobody would go near
it because we were pretty sure it was booby-
trapped. We had to leave it out there and
unfortunately, dogs started going over there. At
one point there were four or five dogs around
this body, eating this body and the Bradley was
there. And I saw the turret start swinging in that
direction, I thought, I'm curious to see where

this is going to go. The guy turned the 240 on it and just mowed the dogs down. Not a single one of them made it. The problem was, even with four or five dead dogs there, more dogs would show up eventually and start trying to eat those. At one point we literally had a pile of dogs around one Iraqi in the middle of the street. It really started to stink after while. We were pinned down on that rooftop for about three days by snipers and I eventually winchestered [ran out of ammo] an AC-130 one night on several targets.

We eventually got back to the TOC and had an MRE cookout. ROMADs being the way they are; started a huge fire. I had a bunch of reactive armor plates off our Bradley, we'd been hit by an RPG, so I was taking chunks of C4 out of them and throwing them into the fire. They burn just fine; as long as you don't add pressure you're all right. So, we all just sat around and told war stories. We get back to Camp Fallujah, getting ready to go back to Camp Victory and convoy out there in two days. The Marine General did what he said, he pulled in two huge-assed CONEX's of beer and we all sat out there and had a couple of cold ones. He told us we all did an awesome job in taking the city back. It just blows my mind now to see how the city is back under enemy control again. It really interests me, I was in the city for about fourteen days fighting, it was pretty epic.

Joe continues to serve and deploy. He is currently serving in a high vis staff position and goes to bat for his community on a daily basis. The master of multi-tasking, he was until recently the owner operator of a full up bar and barbeque while expertly fulfilling his duties as a squadron operations superintendent.

Vet: *"Kinko"*
Setting: *The Green Turtle Bar, Hampton, VA. Kinko and I would meet at one of several bars situated prior to the onramp to I64 West, which is what he took home from work everyday. We'd meet once a week or so for a beer or two to catch up and trade stories on how we were doing and life in general. During one of those meets, he told me this story.*
Drinks: *Kinko – Sweetwater 420 Extra Pale Ale, I had the same. We drank our beers at a pub table near the bar, when Kinko told me this "short" story...*

Story: There was this one time when I was flying with the Iraqi Air Force, actually training them to fly. This is funny now that it's over, and I lived through it. I had a mission to fly with an Iraqi pilot from Baghdad to Basrah. This is 2010. We were flying the Iraqi version of our MC-12s, the King Air 350. They used it for whatever they wanted to use it for. One of the pilots needed to get down to Basra to take leave, so we worked this into a training mission.

Let me back up a second, when the Iraqi pilots trained initially in Iraq they flew T-6s, when they were training for the King Air 350 the got to go to the States for that training. Part of that training included a simulator. The sim had a weird aspect to it. You had to go into the sim's brain, the FMS and tell it where it was, so that the students could take off, flying their simulated training mission, reinitialize and redo, over and over. Since the student pilots had to fly a lot of sims, over and over, it became a habit. So, the problem was, they really got used to doing that as part of flying. Since our training was geared specifically to train Iraqi pilots to fly in Iraq, the default airfield was Baghdad. Once we found out the students were doing this as a habit we beat it out of them. Well, we *thought* we had it fixed. So we took off out of Baghdad and had an uneventful flight down to Basra, which if you're familiar with the geography sits in a narrow strip between Kuwait and Iran. Now it's time to head back to Baghdad.

We take off out of Basrah, it's nighttime and I'm taxiing for takeoff. My Iraqi copilot reaches over and hits the magic button and initializes our position – to Baghdad. I don't realize he's done that. So, now the aircraft thinks it's in Baghdad, when we're actually in Basra, a couple hundred miles south, on the borders of Iran and Kuwait. So, we take off to the east, I still don't notice the navigation problem, turn back to the northeast and climb to 10,000 feet, in order to be able to talk to a controller. At this point, until we talk to a controller, we're on our own, it's night and I don't know it yet, but we're heading toward Iran. I look down at my moving map display and it shows we're at Baghdad. Now it hits me, I realize we're a mere miles from Iran; this would not be good, an Iraqi King Air, with an American Pilot flying into Iran, so I immediately turn to what I figure is my safest direction, West! I now know I won't cross into Iran and I figure out what happened. "You stupid fuck!" I yell at the copilot, "You know you're not supposed to do that!" So, he, his name was Mustafa, he says, "We must level! We must level!" I start thinking, I know I won't go into Iran or Kuwait and I don't want to land back in Basrah or I'll be sleeping in an Iraqi soldiers billet. So, I tell the co, "You need to unfuck this!" He looks at me with this dazed look on his face. There was no way to fix it airborne; it was a weight on wheels function. I told him, "Look in the books, I don't need you for copilot duties!" He climbs in the back and starts rifling through the manuals. After some time, he comes back, "I can't fix." I looked at him for a few seconds and he turned around and jumped back in the back into the books. We had maps onboard, but we never used them. If you can picture this, this is a glass-cockpit aircraft, all high tech modern gauges and instruments, but now I've got to go old school. I break out a map and find a VOR and tune it in. Once I had that setup, I knew we could get back. I tell Mustafa it's now time for him to fly. Again, I get the deer in the headlights look. But, then he takes the controls; he's got the aircraft. He's struggling with all of this, all the way back to Baghdad. I was mad so I was happy to let him struggle. He's sweating bullets. By the time we got in the vicinity of Baghdad he was spent. He flew the whole approach, but I helped him at that point. I had had enough retribution.

What could have been a disaster, we later laughed about. Not for quite a while, but we both did laugh about it.

Kinko recently retired and had a long and great career as a pilot and an Air Liaison Officer. He is still involved in training pilots and currently lives in Europe with his great family.

****

Vet: *"JJ"*
Setting: *Poquoson Bar*
Drinks: *Wild Turkey and Coke, Sam Adams Lager*

Story: "In the early summer of 2007 I was deployed to Balad, Iraq, as an AC-130 aircraft commander. I had a very experienced crew with me. We were flying at night and sleeping during the days as we usually did. One night we were given a mission prior to takeoff, which is unusual for the AC-130. Normally we'd launch and then go figure out what we were going to do once we got airborne. This time we were supporting a Special Ops element that was going after a high value target, which was the cell that had shot down a CH-46 the previous year that was filled with Marines. So, they were very interested in a kill or capture mission on these guys. This was also a little bit unusual, normally they would just go after capture. This time it was no one comes off the objective.

We launched on the mission and linked up with the ground party on the radio. They had inserted and were making their movement toward the objective, which a remote complex, kinda like a farmhouse with a fenced in courtyard outside and a house in the middle, very common in Iraq. The house had a rooftop that access from a staircase inside the house. When we got overhead and got in touch with the unit, we noticed there were guys sleeping on the rooftop, which was not unusual in the summer in Iraq and there was also some people we saw sleeping in the courtyard, which was a little bit unusual. You usually didn't see that, but they were going to sleep outside they would sleep on the rooftop. We talked to the leader of the Special Ops team and let them know what we saw. They copied. When they assaulted the objective, they did get into a minor firefight with some of the guys that were in the courtyard. They had alerted the guys up on the rooftop that something was going on. They were able to capture the dudes that were down in the courtyard, other than the ones they had shot and were getting ready to go into the building, when one of my sensor operators, who was a very experienced Master Sergeant, saw an explosion on the rooftop. I saw it out the window of the AC-130 and the sensor operator saw it on his IR sensor. I assumed that they had thrown a grenade up on top of the roof. My sensor operator, Rich, said no, he thought that might have been a suicide vest, and I'm seeing body parts everywhere now and you see that in IR as the body parts are spread all over the place when they start to cool down, that's what he noticed. Immediately the navigator related down to the team chief and the JTAC we were working with that there may be suicide vests up there. That kind of changed the whole calculus for the team going in. That was something that, despite hearing about suicide vests often, you don't really see them that often. They were very cautious going into the objective. They assaulted the lower part of the building and captured some guys that were inside the house and from there it got interesting. We could tell from the ground party that there was a pretty good fight going into the house, they had managed to capture or kill anybody who gave them resistance down there, but now there was the issue of the rooftop.

Now what we saw when the fighting started, right before actually, was two individuals detonated themselves. It was a little bit of buffoonery on the insurgent's part. They thought that somebody had come up onto the rooftop, is what we surmised, and they thought it was time to blow up the suicide vests, one guy went off and they other guy says, hey he just went off, it's my turn too. He blew himself up. A third guy had jumped off the roof, he must have said I'm not so much into this suicide thing and started E and E'ing out through the orchard, a grove that surrounded the compound. We were keeping an eye on this guy and there's a saying in the gunship, 'You can run, but you're gonna die tired.' On this mission that was kinda proven true for this mission. So we ended up talking to the ground party and they said, Hey we're getting ready to go up on the roof and then we saw the most disturbing thing I had seen in my entire time in the service. The door of the rooftop, what we call a cupola, opens and a guy we had not seen prior, because we thought everybody was dead or had jumped off the roof, all of a sudden somebody opens up with a DshK, a heavy machine-gun on the rooftop, on the guy that had walked out of the cupola, and literally cuts him in half. We thought for sure it was one of the team we were covering. So, there was a moment in the aircraft, your gut dropping, thinking, did we just manage to lose a dude on the objective. It turns out that wasn't the case. We called immediately down to the ground party and said, 'Hey, we just saw somebody open up with a heavy machine-gun there.' They said, 'Yeah, they just cut the guy we sent up there to bring the other guys down. They just cut him in half.' At this point the ground party says, '...we've had a enough of this. We're going to go ahead and egress the building and once we're out of here you're cleared to engage the building.' They, one at a time, would run from the building, across the courtyard area to get behind the wall that surrounded this complex where they were safe. Every time a guy would run for that exit, the guy on the rooftop was opening up on his DshK as he ran. We really couldn't engage until those guys were out of there. Six guys that were on the objective managed to egress the building and they finally told us that they were clear. At which point from the gunship we engaged the building and went after this guy and anybody else that we might not have seen on there. One of the things that stands out in my mind, when we shot this guy on the rooftop, he himself was wearing a suicide vest, he exploded and was thrown, probably about forty meters off of the rooftop, which even with the big gun is not going to happen. But, it was actually the smaller gun we hit him with. So, the ground party was safe, they had captured a few of the guys on the objective, but they had also taken out some of the guys that they weren't able to capture. We did go after the guy that had managed to crawl away and get him out in one of the fields.

The most satisfying part of the mission was the next day when we showed up to fly our next day's mission and we received a call from the team we were supporting, from their Lieutenant team leader, to tell us that if we hadn't recognized that there were suicide vests involved at the objective, that he would have lost guys on the objective. He had no doubt in his mind about that. So, in a way, we walked out of there feeling like we really had done the job well and the thing that stuck with me over the years, was if one guy had been doing that we would not have been as effective. There was a senior sensor operator that recognized the key ingredient there. I had a very good FCO, Fire Control Officer who was able to calmly assess the situation and assign the appropriate responsibilities to the crew in the battle management center to engage the target. I also had a navigator who was extremely calm on the radio talking to the ground party when there was pandemonium on the ground. That was another thing that was brought up by the team leader, '...if the guy talking to us on the radio hadn't been that calm, we probably wouldn't have kept on with the mission...' Great news story all the way along. The other piece of that that has always stuck with me, we were a very experienced crew. The little area we had in the trailers we all lived in, they had names for them, like the eagle's nest, or something, I found out later, they used to call it 'Assisted Living,' over there because of my age and the age of a bunch of the guys on the crew, who were all more senior guys. I remember the next morning walking around. I just couldn't get to sleep, which wasn't normal. All of us had shot countless times. I ran into Rich, the sensor operator who was the key, one of the absolute keys to the success and our reaction was like, 'Wow, that shit just happened.' We both kinda just said, 'Yeah, that was something else.' Then we went to bed and pressed on. In thirty-two years of service, looking back at it, that was by far the most satisfying thing I'd ever done and I'll carry with me being proudest of in all my years of service.

JJ continued his career as an AC-130 pilot, having also flown RC-135s. He was a multi-tour commander in the Tactical Air Control Party mission area, commanding at home and in combat. He wasn't able to avoid becoming what he always despised; he is currently serving as a paper pushing staff office at a Major Command Headquarters, but retains his sanity by playing guitar and singing in various pubs and bars, Irish and otherwise, around the area.

****

Vet: *"JT"*
Setting: *By the pool at Mike B's house in Northern Virginia, the day after the premier of RANGE 15*
Drinks: *JT and I were both having ice cold Pacificos, four apiece so far.*

Story: "In 2005 I was up in Mosul, at FOB Marez and we had the last flight of F-14s before they were going to be decommissioned. So, everyday we had F-14s and we had a constant air patrol over Marez too. What that did as far as JTACs, we didn't have to do mission planning, because we always had CAS ready to go in the arc; we would roll every day and there would be something in the sky that we'd be talking to.

One of the pilots had worked a deal with us to actually go on a couple ground missions to get a feel for it then go back to the jet and fly for us. So, he flies into Diamond Back Airfield, which is right there on the south of Marez. And we planned this all out for his pickup. So we pick him up with the TACP Stryker, we got an Army driver, an Army gunner and an Army TC and three TACPs inside of it; myself, this guy John N. and this guy Chris D. We arrive down at Diamond Back to pick him up and drop the ramp. We drop the ramp and we're real adamant, 'Hey sir, we've got a mission, we're late, we're late, we're late – we gotta get you in...' He's got the typical Interceptor body armor with a World War Two helmet. We hand him a rifle and we're like, 'We gotta go! We gotta go!' and he's flustered. He's like, 'Oh my God, oh my God!' and jumps into the back of the Stryker. We slam the ramp on the Stryker and we start to drive. The drive just from the airfield up to our part of the FOB is fifteen minutes. So, we're taking turns and it's bumpy and when you're in the belly of that Stryker, you've got no clue. So, at the time, I'm the 240 gunner on the back and the JTAC is sitting out of the other hatch. So, this guy is essentially in the belly of this by himself and everybody else is sticking out of a hatch. We all know what's going on and everything, so as we get up to the top of Marez we head to the range on Marez where we're test firing. The rest of the platoon of Strykers is there, they know what we're doing. We're talking to them on the radio and everything. This guy can't hear, he doesn't know what's going on. He's just down there by himself, just sitting there with gun just rocking around, with his helmet that's two sizes too big for him. We all yell at each other, 'Outside! Outside!' playing as if we're leaving the wire, like we were all notifying each of it. Then I peek down, 'Alright, we're in the city now!' And he's like, 'Oh God!' and we'd turned all the monitors off inside, otherwise you could see everything if you were watching the monitors. Again, we're all talking back and forth to each other as if the mission was happening, 'Lead Truck turning, lead truck turning!' we're yelling everything back and forth. As we get to the range we halt and I start screaming and unloading with the 240, and the other TACP slews the .50 Cal and starts opening up with the .50 Cal. And all the guys, the platoon that's already there, they're throwing rocks at the Stryker, 'Ding! Ding! Ding!' we're ducking – 'Ah God!' This guy is ghost-white, we're firing, then I come down and I'm like, 'Alright! We've gotta dismount!' and I drop the ramp. And he's like, 'No! No! No! No! No!' and I grab him by the armor and we run out – and the whole platoon is sitting there just laughing there asses off and they start clapping and he's like 'No!

No! No! Uh, ahh... I hate you guys! I hate you guys!'

He went out for three more days. He went out on a combat mission with us and got to see the ground fight. But, that joke we played on him was priceless!

So, again, I'm back at Marez, I'm part of the 1st of the 17th, Buffaloes, was their nickname, the 172nd Stryker Brigade. We're in the HHC, the headquarters element with the commander and the S3 and everything. So, the commander has a platoon in his PSD of Strykers, so, it's four Strykers we travel with every time we go on a patrol or KLE or anything – we got the four Strykers. One of those was the TACP Stryker. Well, the platoon sergeant of that element, he was kinda salty. He was younger, but he liked to have an attitude against the Air Force guys. So, what do we do – we like to push the buttons and start fucking with him. We started by putting a dead fish from the chow hall in his heater vent. It was really cold at that time. It took about four days until the smell really started to just crush his room. I don't know if we got tattled on, it was unspoken, but he knew the war was with us. So, one morning we go to go on our mission and we can't get out of our hooch, because he had stacked sandbags all the way up to the ceiling against our door. So, we just yelled, 'Don't worry, we got power and Playstation in here, we don't gotta go on the mission, we'll just stay here! Have fun trying to get air coverage.' So, the commander actually told him, actually made him and his guys undo the sandbags, so it was almost like, that joke, that prank backfired on him and he had to do more work. So, after that we knew we had to step it up. But, we wanted to be strategic about it, so what we'd done is put Stryker jacks underneath the rear of his CHU, because these were all on cinder blocks. And then every day we would click the jacks about four clicks. We let this go on for about a week or two and every time we would meet in front of his room before we would go on a mission, that was a daily thing for us, he would start sitting in his room, then stand and lean. He'd put a pen down on his desk and it would start to roll, and he'd look at it, 'This things fucked up.' We just kept clicking it until finally all his stuff fell over and he found the jacks. That was our war, we just kept going back and forth; there was always something new."

JT transitioned to the Air National Guard. He is still a full up Joint Terminal Attack Controller and a full up veteran entrepreneur; President of Article 15 Clothing, Vice President of Black Rifle Coffee, Executive Producer at MattBest11X and star of the recent independent hit movie, Range 15.

****

Vet: *"Marty"*
Setting: *Still at Mike B's a little later by his pool at his house in Northern Virginia, the day after the premier of RANGE 15*
Drinks: *Marty and I were both having Pacificos. He'd just gotten there; I was way ahead.*

Story: "This was my very first deployment, in July of 2006, 1st Battalion, 75th Ranger Regiment. We were at the MSS in BIAP. Before they moved everyone over to Baghdad they had the MSS [mission support site] right next to Saddam's palace. Basically, ten mansions to the right, ten mansions to the left that were for his cabinet and the ten mansions to the right were like the SOF compound. We had a great deployment. Literally this mansion, each squad had its own private suite, each with a bathroom and everything. We had our own swimming pool with a diving board. We built a shoot house out in back to train during the day, we had bar-b-que grills, and a volleyball court and a pool. So, it was a pretty cool deployment. Not as cool if you're the brand new guy on your first deployment. The pool just provided different opportunities to scuff you up if you fucked up.

So, summer 2006, this is right after they got Zarqawi. This was the task force's main effort for a while at that point and we got there right after that, like a week later. We were reorienting ourselves to what's next. We devoted all of our resources to Zarqawi, we got him; now what? We still did, I think, geez, it must have been at least a hundred missions in that hundred day rotation. Didn't go out every single night, but there were a lot of nights we were doing two or three follow-ons. So, this was one of those nights, or a couple of nights in Baghdad – long nights. I was one of two new guys. They would rotate us, one week I would be a Stryker gunner and he would go out as an assaulter, and then we'd switch and I'd go out as an assaulter and he'd be the Stryker gunner. This was my week to be the Stryker gunner. So we go out, we have this long night and the driver's also a pretty new guy as well and the TC [track commander] is like a junior team leader, something like that. We go out and I honestly don't remember what we did that night. There was nothing too memorable, we got some bad guys; I don't what exactly though now.

But, we get in and it's just getting to be daybreak and we're all tired, we're smoked. My TC jumps out and says, 'Alright, go take the Stryker to get fueled.' So, I'm going to TC the Stryker over to the fuel point, so, not a big deal, not even a mile down the road. So, we've got this other kid, I'll leave his name out of it, he's the driver. I just pop open the hatch for the TC, then I say, 'Ramp up, let's go,' he comes back with 'Roger.' The right way to do it, by the book, the FM [field manual] way to do it is, when you say, 'Ramp up,' you as the TC stick your head down and look to ensure the ramp has come up. You may see where I'm going with this. He says, 'Roger,' and we go, because we've done this a hundred times, this is not the first week of deployment, we're halfway, if not two thirds of the way through the deployment at this point, been doing this for a minute, so you trust that when you tell somebody to put the ramp up, that they put the ramp up. We take off and I think we get about a hundred yards down the road before I just casually look behind me to see if the other Strykers have pulled out and I see like a trail of like six guys sprinting down the road after us. I'm like, 'Hey, stop, stop, stop.' I duck down and I tell him, 'Ok, put the ramp down.' And there's nothing, like radio silence. Then I see why, when I duck down and see the ramp is fucking down. You've got to be kidding me. I'm the new guy – this is not going to be good. I see now that every single one of these six or seven guys that are chasing after me is either a tabbed Spec 4 or a team leader. There's no hiding this, there's no covering this up, there's no paying off your fellow private Ranger buddies with a case of beer to fucking keep their mouths shut about this. This is going to be a bad day.

They tell me to get the hell off the Stryker, of course. They tell the other guy to get the hell out of the truck. They hop in and they tell us to start bear crawling back to the compound. So, we're bear crawling down the road heading back to the MSS and this is just the start of the day. We were already coming off a long night of missions and things like that, and this is going to get worse before it gets better. I said to the other guy, 'What the fuck, why didn't you put the ramp up?' I'm starting to now think this might be more serious. As the TC this is ultimately my responsibility, you know. This could get bad, because if the cage on the Stryker is damaged. I'm sitting there thinking in my private mind, they could do like a statement of charges against me. I'm making like $700 a pay check here, I'm pretty sure I can't afford to pay for new cage armor for a Stryker. I'm thinking am I going to get Chaptered [refers to which chapter of the Army Reg you situation is being governed by – can lead to discharge], RFS'ed [released for standards]. So, we bear crawl back to the compound and immediately start getting scuffed up in the pea rocks outside. My squad leader comes up, 'What the fuck? Get in the squad room.' He said, 'Don't worry, you'll be back out, I just have to talk to you. Ok, what happened?' I told him the TC, who was also in our squad hopped out and told me to take it over to the fuel point, so I told the driver to put the ramp up, and that truthfully, I didn't duck down to look, because honestly, we never do that. When you say 'Ramp up,' and they say, 'Roger,' you assume that the ramp is up. And he's like, 'Yeah, you should have checked.' And then he calls in the original TC and goes, 'Why the fuck do you have your gunner taking the Stryker to the fuel point instead of yourself?' The TC is directly in charge of me, so you know how shit rolls downhill. So, now he's doing pushups over there. This is an embarrassment for everybody. We're out on that main road in front of the compound, you've got a SIF platoon on one side, you got the SAS over here, you got a squadron, you got all these guys that saw me driving down the road, and they know, those guys are Rangers, so this is an embarrassment to the Regiment, that's the way my squad leader and the platoon sergeant saw it. So, he's obviously not happy, but he knows what happened. I don't know if there any empathy for me there or not, as far as, well technically he did tell the guy... I don't know. So, I was back outside with the other guy. We got scuffed up for the majority of the afternoon. Then they told us to go get chow, drink some water and get the fuck back here. By this point, it's already starting to get late in the afternoon. This was a day that was longer or as long as any sort of day that I would have gone in RIP, during selection, or something like that. There was no mercy whatsoever. Again, coming after a long night as it was.

Now they said, 'Ok, you're going to guard the shit trailer. The bathroom inside, we could piss in them, but we couldn't shit in them, we had to go out to the trailer out front to actually shit. So, they said, 'You're going to guard the shit trailer, in full kit, all night long and you're going to verify everyone's security badge as they go to take a shit.' They were doing this so that we'd just piss off everyone that came by us, and they'd make us do push ups for asking them for a security badge to go take a shit. So, I go in and start putting on all my kit, as if you were going on a mission. I'm putting eye pro on, making sure my batteries are operational, checking my PEC 2 [rifle scope], cause the thing was, if we did actually roll out on a mission you need to be ready to go.

Again, shit rolls downhill, so the original TC who was told to do pushups by the squad leader, he didn't really get scuffed up, probably 'twenty-five and recover' and counseled, or something like that, like, 'Don't be an idiot.' Be he comes out and says, 'Hey, pretty sure you're going to wear the Skedco [rescue stretcher] tonight too, and why don't you go ahead and take the Hooley [breaching tool] too and just in case we need to breach something really heavy, take the sledge as well.' Son of a bitch – so I go out there and this is after being scuffed up all day long, after missions all night long and there's the other guy and he's getting told the same thing. We get out there and we have our nods off and they were like, 'Nope, nods down, you're going to look through nods all night too.' They told us we were going to be out there all night; we were out there for about three hours. And it was just as they said, we had to ask for security badges, and I'm pretty sure they went around and told everybody, 'Hey I'm pretty sure you need to go take a shit,' so the word got around. So, they all start coming out, I ask for the security badge and they're like, 'Yeah, fuck you, why don't you start doing some pushups while I go grab my security badge.' That lasted about three hours until the PL came out. He was aware of the Stryker incident, but I'm not sure he was aware of everything, he was like, 'Alright guys, I'll go talk to your squad leader, we're embarrassing ourselves more than we already embarrassed ourselves.' Now I'm thinking, oh shit, now I'm being told to go in by the PL. You're gonna be told to go in, it better be by one of your guys, not the PL, you know? So, son of a bitch, but we came in at that point, and we get the, 'Who the fuck told you to come in?' I told them, 'Captain C.,' so, they said, 'Ok,' and right at that point I think a mission was coming down, so they said, 'Ok, make sure you go get hydrated again,' and all that stuff and we did go out again that night, just one I think. That was probably one of the longest thirty-six hours of my life – competing for first or second longest thirty-six hour period, because there was another thing that happened that same exact deployment, it was the whole platoon and it was just a big mess. That's my story.

Marty left the Army but remains active with and supports vets and vet ventures. He is Executive Producer at Cinema Seventy Five and the way he states it, a Husband, father, son, brother, author, writer, producer, entrepreneur, veteran, and traveling man.

****

Vet: *Dude*
Setting: *At home, having a beer with best friend*
Drinks: *Beer*

Story: "It was early 2008. I was the Corps ALO to XVIII Airborne Corps headquartered at Camp Victory, Baghdad, Iraq. As the senior ALO (Air Liaison Officer) in Iraq I commanded all of the US Air Force air integration support to the US Army ground forces. Part of my routine was going to the daily Chief of Staff huddle, to which I'd been to about a million. I had finished PT for the morning, gone to the chow hall for breakfast and then headed over to Al Faw Palace for the meeting. III Corps and XVIII Airborne Corps had just RIP'ed a while back and LTG Austin was in the seat as the MNC-I commander. He was a great leader and a good dude. I had gone over a month or so in advance of the XVIIIth because the Air Force was desynched with the Army on rotations. I was LTG Odierno's ALO for a while before the XVIIIth came in to replace the IIIrd. When LTG Austin got on station there was a reception, welcoming him into command. When I walked through the line and it was my turn to shake his hand, he said, 'Ah, there's my ALO, great to see you,' or something like that, and it really felt like he meant it. I know he did.

The XVIIIth had been operating for a few months, running some offensive operations and a lot of stability and sustainment ops. The news at the Chief of Staff huddle was, Prime Minister Maliki decided to send five Iraqi divisions to retake Basra. What none of us really knew at the time was that Basra was actually under insurgent control for quite some time, a really long time. The Mahdi militia owned the city. The British had responsibility for the province and their area of control had been shrinking. The Mahdi militia had started using Explosively Formed Penetrators (EFPs), which wreaked havoc on the Brits and forced them to fall back inside their bases, where they were then attacked with mortars and rockets. In December 2007 the British turned over control of the city to the Iraqis. I learned later that after being pushed back from the city the Brits tried to retake the city center and had gotten really scuffed up. They lost a tank, took multiple casualties and fell back to the airport, which was the state of affairs when the Corps got involved.

So, I headed into the Chief of Staff meeting expecting ops normal. Right off the bat, the Chief said, 'LTG Austin is going to deploy the Corps TAC to Basra, under the command of Major General Flynn to assist the British Battle Group there in supporting the Iraqi Army's offensive to retake Basra.' This was news to all of us. The Fire Support Coordinator for the Corps, Pete Edmonds, told me I was expected to move out with the TAC to coordinate air support. Sounded good to me, but it was a bit of surprise. I was moving out the next morning, but I was commander of the Air Support Operations Group, which was basically all of the TACP and Weather Airmen in Iraq. I had a good deputy, who could keep things going, so what the fuck.

The first thing I had to do was figure out what I needed to set up a C2 node down there in order to control all the close air support we'd need to support a city assault with five divisions, plus special ops and a British Battle Group. I figured the first thing I'd do would be to take one of the shifts from the ASOC, the Air Support Operations Center, the team that dynamically controlled the flow, integration and tasking of aircraft and air support for Iraq. I had three eight-hour shifts, so I adjusted to two twelve-hour shifts. This gave me an eight-man crew. Also, for some fortuitous reason, I was aware that the Marine DASC was being under-utilized. I had talked to the Captain in charge and he agreed to chop me a slice of the DASC to assist with my C2 set up. I continued to work issues in getting everything set up throughout the day. I had a Group to take care of, but I also understood this was the priority, and this was a fight. Not that we weren't fighting constantly, but this was a battle to retake a city. It doesn't get much better than that.

I put together the team and flew into Basra Airport on or about 20-21 March 2008. We flew in at night and eventually figured out where we were billeted. The British had been there awhile so they'd learned some lessons. The tent we stayed in was something like a GP large. Just before we'd gotten there that tent had been hit by a mortar round and I believe several Brits were killed. Each of the billets was an individual bunker made up of sandbag walls with an opening on one side. A metal plate about eight feet long, three feet wide and about three quarters of an inch thick was placed on top. On top of that was another layer of sandbags. It felt like a coffin when you crawled inside.

The next morning was my first meeting with MG Flynn. He held a staff meeting to see where we stood. I laid out the air support plan, told him I melded an ASOC slice with a DASC slice, got E-2 support off the career just off the coast and had sorties dedicated to our operations from now to mission complete. He seemed impressed. When I finished my brief with, 'Sir, that's all I've got,' he responded with, 'That's enough.' I'll fast forward to my opinion of MG Flynn. Working with, actually, working for him was one of my career highlights. The responsibility we were all given to ensure the Iraqi Army succeeded and retook the city was amazing, but then he gave me the responsibility and the authority to carry out the air support campaign. As far as airstrikes were concerned he gave that to me, basically giving me his ground commander authority. He tasked me to kill all the enemy indirect fire capability, or we wouldn't be able to push into the city and conduct clearing operations. In short, MG Flynn; awesome leader and warrior.

Part of what we had to accomplish was linking up and synching up with the Iraqi leadership. That was General Flynn's job, but he took me and his Army deputy with him. It was almost nightly after the first engagement that we flew into the BOC - the Basra Operations Center. On the first night we flew in in a couple of Blackhawks, it was sporty. I looked down at the city and you could see tracer fire and explosions. Either a rocket or an RPG passed just underneath us, to me it looked like between the skid and the body of the helicopter. We land at the BOC get out and go into an old, dark building. We descend a flight of stairs and it's like, holy shit, this is like Heart of Darkness. Both sides of the narrow passageways were lined with Iraqi soldiers seeking cover. You could barely make anything out, except their faces and their eyes. We snaked our way through the bowels of that ancient building. At one point we came across our Fires Chief who had been sent to work targeting with the Iraqis. Looking at all of those faces, all staring back at us like we were aliens, then the Chief's face comes into view. He was a trooper. He was making things happen. He joined us as we ascended into the BOC.

Once we got up out of the basement we preceded to Gen Mohan's office. Gen Mohan had been put in charge of the Basra Operations Command in August of 2007 and controlled the 14th and 10th Iraqi Divisions. We waited for a couple of minutes, but then the doors opened and we all went in. We had an interpreter. Gen Mohan greeted MG Flynn and through the interpreter, they exchanged pleasantries. The greetings circled around the room and everybody met everybody. But, when I was introduced to Gen Mohan, either they specified I was in the USAF or that I was controlling the air support, but he changed his demeanor, and grasped my outstretched hand with both of his and through the interpreter said, 'You're the one we've been cheering for.' To me, it was obvious that the Iraqis appreciated US airpower. He'd personally been subjected to it twice during Desert Storm and OIF. He knew where the asymmetric advantage lay and he wanted to show his appreciation, and he wanted some.

The battle, with the Iraqi operation name of 'Charge of the Knights,' began on 24 March 2008. The city was sealed off, roadblocks were set up and curfews were established. Al Sadr warned that if his militia were targeted he'd retaliate. We had US air support and three British AS90 self-propelled howitzers from the British Battle Group, and MiTTs [Military Transition Teams – US teams created to assist the Iraq maneuver units] embedded with each of the Iraqi Brigades. The MiTTs were the Military Transition Teams comprised of US soldiers across several specialties that advised and assisted their Iraqi counterparts. We also had US and Iraqi Special Ops forces. The Iraqi SOF were squared away. I had US and Brit JTACs with some of the key MiTTs with the lead Iraqi units and a couple defending the BOC and a couple helping me run the C2 from the Brit HQ at the airport. Early in the morning on the 25th the Iraqis entered the city and started clearing operations. They immediately faced fierce resistance.

Over the next few days the fighting intensified. We were taking incoming hits from rockets and mortars. MG Flynn told me to kill all of the enemy's indirect fire systems. I focused our strike aircraft, using the Brits organic ISR and our US Reapers and Predators to find targets and take them out. We also used the weapons off the platforms to directly take out enemy positions and when we found them, the mortar and rocket teams. After a few days of indecisive fighting the Iraqis set up for a more deliberate attack. We were going to use a few CAS sorties and a barrage from the AS90 Braveheart 155mm's to lay down some prep fires. We had the details worked out so the timing would be close between the artillery and bombs. Everybody was hoping the firepower demonstration would demoralize the enemy and spur on the Iraqis. We're about 30 minutes out and I should have been hearing from the 2x F-16s that were going to start the show. I didn't hear anything for another few minutes, then my 'oh shit' sensor started going off. I picked up the phone and called the Senior Offensive Duty Officer (SODO) at the CAOC. He picks up the phone and gives me one of those lengthy...

"Hello sir or ma'am, this is Colonel So and So, this is an unsecure line, how can I help you...?" We're running out of time, so I'm a little impatient,

'Hey Colonel So and So, got any SA on the 2x F-16s that are supposed to have checked in with me about 20 minutes ago?"

He comes back with, 'Hey Dude, how you doing? No, not tracking, hang on a sec, let me check." I look over my shoulder at MG Flynn, who's at his seat watching the video feeds, he says, "Hey ALO, where's the Air Force?"

"Checking on it sir." I'm still not

worried because I figure, if there was a problem, they would have let me know.

"Uh, Dude?" Colonel So and So is back on the line. "Yeah, uh, looks like they're still on the ground at Balad."

'What? You gotta be shitting me. When did you guys figure on telling me that? We've got pre-assault fires scheduled in ten minutes, then we're assaulting the city 20 minutes after that,' I ask, trying not to raise my voice.

"Uh, yeah, they're not going to make it."

'No Shit,' I said. 'You got anything you can retask?'

"Uh, let me check," comes back Colonel So and So. "Uh, yeah, we can shift a couple of F-18s scheduled for about a half an hour deck launch over to you to cover the CAS vuls, but ain't gonna help you with your fires." I guess I put the phone down a little firmer than I should have, which caught MG Flynn's attention.

"Hey ALO, nothing more reliable than Artillery, it's never late."
The general was a Marine Artillery officer so anytime, like all other red-leg arty guys, they get a chance to shit on air power, they'll take it. The general appreciated what we were doing, but it was in his DNA. So, the arty shoots, which was great, but not as inspiring I figure as a pile of 2000-lbers.

The assault starts and we've got a couple of CAS engagements, then our compound on the airport starts taking mortar fire. A few rounds hit close to our HQ and the Brit Arty guys are working up a counter-fire solution. We get the coordinates and pass them to a Predator. This is all actually to the best of my recollection, as far as the sequence and timing and all that. But we get Predator eyes on the mortar team, they're right downtown. It's a family affair, dad's working the aiming, mom's dropping the rounds and sonny's bringing the rounds to mom, they're hanging rounds like crazy. We get the Predator lined up and through the JTAC at the desk I give the cleared hot call. Nothing happens. Ok. Retransmit. Nothing happens. They continue to launch rounds and one hits the edge of the compound and we find out later that it kills a Brit soldier. We're now chatting with the Predator pilot, asking why he didn't fire after the cleared hot call. He relays that he saw a kid, so he held fire. Fuck.

The battle goes on. A couple of the Brit JTACs got wounded, one after the other on two consecutive nights. One got hit in the face with the frag from an RPG. He was up on top of the BOC. I replaced him and the next guy got hit. Now I pull one of our JTACs out of our TOC and send him into the BOC. He did a great job and got some pretty good action. We're still catching rounds on the assaulters and into our compound and HQ so I'm still focused on killing the indirect fire teams.

One night we see a vehicle, actually looked like a '60s Buick winding its way through town near the river. We're tracking it with overhead ISR and watch it come to a stop. A couple of guys get out of the car and start unloading stuff out of the trunk. Looked like a mortar tube, rounds and a couple of rockets. They load stuff into a pair of boats, two guys per boat. They start traversing the river heading toward our guys on the opposite shore. That spot was previously identified to be a POO - Point of Origin of some previous mortar attacks. I check with the JTAC to see what was on station. MG Flynn had given me strike authority so it was my call. The boats were about half way across. JTAC passes we've got a flight of AH-64s, Apaches on station. The JTAC makes contact and turns and looks back at me. I told him to pass him a nine-line and stand by; they receive and acknowledge. Now they're about three quarters of the way across. We've got no choice at this point. If those weapons get to the other side, we'll have them raining down on us any minute. First pass lead makes a running gun run and hits both guys in the lead boat, cuts one in half along with the boat. Number two makes a pass and cuts the second boat in half and sinks it. The two guys in that boat desperately swim for the shore and make it to the reeds and grab on and hunker down. The IR shows them clearly. There's no place for them to hide. I ask the Brit maneuver lead if they've got anybody in the area that can go pick them up, capture them. He said no. I pass to the JTAC to clear the Apaches to finish their attack. They each made a pass and killed them. I'd done this before. I'd controlled strikes on almost every deployment that had the same end result, but this one felt different. I felt sick. I looked at my Chief and I think I talked to him the next day briefly about it and he said all the right stuff. That night when I decided to get some rack time, I didn't have a shift, I just went 'till I couldn't go anymore, I went back to the tent and crawled into my coffin. I had a tough time getting any sleep. I prayed a lot. The next morning I was back at it. There were a lot more events, fights, successes and losses, but, after thirty days we, actually the Iraqis, won and took back Basra.

I think about those guys in the water from time to time. There was nothing they could do against a flight of Apache attack helicopters. They were defenseless. They were the enemy, the Rules of Engagement and Laws of War were clear, but still, I felt like shit about it, and sometimes still do.

Conclusion

Well, you've just read through a century of veteran stories covering eight conflicts. I really hope you enjoyed the journey and feel that you've gotten a glimpse into how some veterans view their service experience. You can tell that their experiences affected each vet differently, but you probably also noticed some common threads. I picked up on a dynamic that was revealed in many of the stories, maybe because I felt the same way. It was how once deployed and overseas doing their duty, many of the veterans became more comfortable with the combat environment then their lives back home. It wasn't that they didn't love and miss their families, or prefer not to get shot at, or be back home, but there is clarity to the combat environment, that you really can't obtain back home. "Normal" life comes with a lot of distractions and competing priorities and demands from many different people. In combat, you've got a clear chain of command, a singular purpose and you're part of a team that relies on you and you on them. Downrange, if you're in charge, your decisions are final; there are no debates, nobody is second-guessing you. If you're a grunt, you're responsibilities are even clearer and you are responsible for the grunt to your left and for the grunt to your right. They are responsible for you and the guy to their left or right. The world becomes and actually is very black and white, very simple. Life at home is complicated. Life downrange is simple, all you've got to worry about it getting killed. That's easy.

Reading through the stories you hopefully came to appreciate the differences in eras and the differences in how the vets told their stories. Someone who grew up in the '20s and '30s will always have a different perspective than someone who grew up in the '80s and 90's. You also may have felt the passion and release emanating from the telling of stories that aren't often, if ever told. I did. Not all of the stories were classic war stories, but that's not what this book was really about. Most of the stories may be about combat, but life in the military presents its unique challenges, even when nobody's shooting at you. For the first 10 years of my 30-year career, we lost many more of our comrades to training accidents than combat. It's a dangerous and sometimes lonely profession. There are always extended periods away from home, birthdays, graduations and anniversaries missed. It's not an easy life and it's a career that the vets, at least over the last nearly forty years, have volunteered to serve in. It's also an experience most vets wouldn't trade. Another aspect of the military you may have picked up on is the power of belonging to a unit. In combat when you're personally faced with a go/no-go decision, you go. You gotta go, you've got no choice. Over the top, out the door, through the door, into the breech you go, because the guy in front of you, next to you, beside you goes. You go. It takes more strength not to, militaries have relied on that fact for thousands of years.

If you're not a vet and you've read this first volume of *There I Was*... thank you. I hope you've enjoyed it and found it interesting and hopefully illuminating. By reading these stories, hearing them as told to you, you've helped us capture forever the stories of these vets and a piece of our history. If you are a vet I hope you felt connected to your fellow vet storytellers and if you want to share your experiences, tell me your story...

www.A15Publishing.com
A15publishinginfo@gmail.com

GLOSSARY OF TERMS

The following is a list of acronyms, abbreviations, terms and weapons systems briefly defined in the order they appeared in the book. If there are any terms, phrases or abbreviations that weren't explained that you'd like more info on drop us a note at the addresses provided above.

1C4 – USAF enlisted forward air controller **AAA** – Anti Aircraft Artillery
AFSOC – Air Force Special Operations Command
ALO – Air Liaison Officer – USAF officer who integrates airpower with ground ops
AO – Area of Operations
AK-47 – 7.62mm Assault Rifle developed by the USSR
ASOG – Air Support Operations Group – USAF unit in charge of subordinate Air Force squadrons who support Army Divisions with airpower expertise and forward air control
AS-90 Braveheart – British self-propelled 155mm cannon system
AT-4 – Infantry Anti-Tank weapon
B-26 – A WWII tactical two engine bomber
B-29 – Long Range Bomber developed/employed during WWII, dropped the A-Bomb
Bangalore Torpedo – demolition device used to breach obstacles
Battalion – (BN) Military organization, approximately 700 troops
BIAP – Baghdad International Airport
BG – Brigadier General – one star
Brigade – (BDE) Military organization, from 3000-5000 troops
C2 – Command and Control
C4 – Plastic Explosive
C-Rations – Canned food for combat troops, less substantial than K-rations
CAOC – Combined Air Operations Center – large

organizational headquarters in charge of all air operations for a large region

CAR-15 – Colt Automatic Rifle

CAS – Close Air Support – aircraft employing weapons close to ground troops

CAV – Cavalry Forces – light armored or airborne

CD – Civil Disturbance

CFACC – Combined Forces Air Component Commander – top officer in charge of airpower

CHU – Containerized Housing Unit – prefabricated housing employed overseas

COIN – Counter Insurgency

Company – (CO) Military organization, approximately 120 troops

COMALF – Commander of Air Lift Forces – Senior officer in charge of air logistics

CONEX – Intermodel Container – metal shipping container

DASC – Direct Air Support Center – Marine air support operations center

Division – (DIV) Military organization, from 20-30,000 troops

D-Day - The first day of an operation (ex: 6 Jun 1944, D-Day for Operation Overlord)

D+ - The number of days after D-Day

DIRMOBFOR – Director of Mobility Forces – Officer in charge of airlift operations

DshK – Russian made heavy machinegun

Dud – Weapon that doesn't detonate

DZ – Drop Zone – area designated for a parachute drop

E-2 – "Hawkeye" US Navy surveillance aircraft

E-(x) – ex E-3, E-4, enlisted rank structure

EBALO – Enlisted Battalion Air Liaison Officer – USAF Airman

FM – Field Manual

FOB – Forward Operating Base

G2 - Army Intelligence section

GEN – General – four star

GP – General Purpose – refers to a large tent

GPS – Global Positioning System – satellite enabled aid to navigation
HEMET – Heavy Expanded Mobility Tactical Truck – vehicle used to transport tanks and tracked vehicles over long distances
HQ – Headquarters
ID'ed – Identified
IR - Infrared
ISR – Intelligence Surveillance and Reconnaissance
IZLID – Infrared Illuminator – used to point out targets to aircraft
JDAM – Joint Direct Attack Munitions (GPS guided bomb)
JOC – Joint Operations Center – same as above, but with multiple services
JSTARS – Joint Surveillance and Target Attack Radar System (E-8 Aircraft)
JTAC – Joint Terminal Attack Controller – forward air controller
K -Rations – Packaged meal for combat troops in first issued in WWII
KIA – Killed in Action
KLE – Key Leader Engagement
Klicks – Abbreviation for Kilometers
LCPV – Landing Craft Vehicle Personnel – boats Marines used to get from transports to the beaches
LTC – Army/Marine abbreviation for rank of Lieutenant Colonel
LTG – Lieutenant General – three star
M60 – US made medium machinegun, .30 caliber
MASH – Mobile Army Surgical Hospital
MG – Major General – two star
MiTT – Military Transition Team – team of US personnel that were imbedded with Iraqi and Afghani forces to assist in training for independent operations
MNC-I – Multi-National Corps – Iraq
MRE – Meals Ready to Eat – modern day K-rations
MSS – Modular Sleep System – sleeping bag
NCO – Non-Commissioned Officer
NVG – Night Vision Goggles

NTC – National Training Center – several large areas in the US for military training

NVA – North Vietnamese Army – conventional communist army of North Vietnam

ODA – Operational Detachment Alpha – Special Forces unit

OPTEMPO – Operations Tempo

POO – Point of Origin – geographic point where an enemy weapon system was fired from (like a mortar)

POW – Prisoner of War

Predator – US designed unmanned aerial vehicle

PT – Physical Training

PZ – Pickup Zone

QRF – Quick Reaction Force – an alert force of combat troops used to rapidly respond to developing situations

Reaper – US unmanned aerial vehicle, much larger and more capable than the Predator

RIP – Relief in Place – a unit taking another unit's place in combat

ROMAD – Radio Operator Maintainer and Driver – legacy term used to describe the USAF Airman who support ground operations

RPG – Rocket Propelled Grenade – grenade launder developed by the USSR

RTO – Radio Telephone Operator – Army radio operator

SAS – Special Air Service – British Special Forces

Satchel Charges – demolition device used to demolish fortifications and breach obstacles developed/employed during WWII

SATCOM – Satellite Communications

Schwack – Parlance for destroy or obliterate

SeaBees – Navy combat engineers, derived from "Construction Battalion"

SOCOM – Special Operations Command

SOF – Special Operations Forces

SP – Shore Police – Navy Cops

Stryker – US military armored vehicle

SWAT – Special Weapons and Tactics Team

TACP – Tactical Air Control Party – USAF element aligned with ground forces

TAC – Tactical Command Post – a smaller command headquarters sent forward from the main command post

TC – Track Commander – soldier in charge of the vehicle

TOC – Tactical Operations Center – headquarters with cross-functional expertise supporting an operation

USO – United Service Organization – established to help troops and families

VC – Viet Cong – communist guerilla organization during Vietnam War